THE
ALL-ANIMAL VET

About the Author

Margareta Shiel travelled to Australia overland from her homeland, Sweden, in 1973 with only a backpack. After three months she arrived in Perth, Western Australia. She worked on several large sheep properties, ran a dairy for five years, and managed a Santa Gertrudis cattle stud for eight years. She was admitted to the five-year veterinary course at Queensland University as a mature age student at age 39. After graduating with honours in 1993, she decided to work as a locum all over Australia and overseas. Her love for nature took her bird- and wildlife-watching to all corners of the globe. She bought a property in southern Tasmania where she started her own veterinary business. She finally retired from vet work in 2024 to transform her property to a wildlife haven, planting hundreds of trees and native plants.

Margareta treating a water buffalo in Tasmania

THE
ALL-ANIMAL VET

Stories from a vet in outback Australia

Margareta Shiel

ASHWOOD
PUBLISHING

Copyright © Margareta Shiel 2025
All rights reserved. Apart from as permitted by Australian copyright law, no part of this work may be reproduced by any means without the permission of the author. Contact the publisher for information.

ISBN-paperback: 978-1-7636921-6-9
ISBN-epub: 978-1-7636921-7-6

Published by Ashwood Publishing, Cradoc, Tasmania.
ashwoodpublishing.com.au
info@ashwoodpublishing.com.au

The work of Ashwood Publishing is nurtured by the beautiful country of the Melukerdee people in the Huon Valley in southern Lutruwita/Tasmania. We acknowledge and pay respect to the traditional owners and their continuing custodianship of this place.

 A catalogue record for this work is available from the National Library of Australia

Contents

About the Author ii
Preface ix
1. Becoming a vet 1
2. My first cow caesar – and in the dark! 3
3. Midget the Chihuahua 13
4. The Blonde Vet 15
5. The so-called "quiet" horse 18
6. General horse behaviour 25
7. Caesar on a wild baldy cow on a Sunday 28
8. Breaking in a buck-jumper 34
9. Talking to deaf ears 38
10. Marcia the draft horse 42
11. My first dog caesar: 2 am and the lights go out 47
12. A hard choice: ethics or heroism? 54
13. Feedlot steers in trouble 58
14. On call all night 63
15. Ungrateful farmers 66
16. The blue-stained overalls 69
17. Port Hedland Vet Surgery: A hard kind of job 72
18. Ticks galore 77
19. The fainting client 79
20. Port Hedland Tourist Bureau: An oasis in Hell 82
21. A trip into the desert 88
22. Monkey Mia, where dolphins meet people 97
23. Cheviot Lodge 99
24. Arrival in Katanning 101
25. What a hillbilly show 108
26. Wyreema Jess 111
27. Mrs Bessen is coming: Take cover! 114
28. A vet's heartache 117
29. The Sawyers 120
30. A learning curve like no other 123
31. Mr Moore's ostriches: You can't win them all 127
32. Horse trials: What could go wrong? 131

33. Losing one of my own horses 135
34. How persistence wins 140
35. The fragility of horses 144
36. Bulldogs in love 149
37. A happy story of a little bird 153
38. Heartbreak again 156
39. Has my cat been poisoned? 158
40. A natural brew for sick sheep 160
41. The things vets have to do 163
42. Don't panic! You can do it! 166
43. A sad day: three euthanasias 169
44. The joys of being a large-animal vet 172
45. Pigs, dogs and corncobs 176
46. A hypochondriac horse or owner? 180
47. Max and the mad cat 183
48. You try, and sometimes you fail 187
49. Sadly, bad accidents do happen 191
50. When you can't trust the owner's story 195
51. Doubting female vets again? 198
52. Rocket the hyper kelpie in pain 202
53. Bluey the ginger cat 204
54. A snowstorm and muddy dogs 207
55. Skip the mystery dog 211
56. Lucky the buffalo 215
57. Dogs and delusions 220
58. A horse jammed under huge logs 224
59. The evil client 230
60. The wake 232
61. Dandy 236

Preface

I WROTE THIS BOOK FROM NOTES I have taken over the years. Its contents are not intended to be taken seriously; nor are its veterinary methods to be taken as instructive by prospective veterinarians. I felt the need to tell my story about a most wonderful, challenging and interesting time of my life. Hopefully it will inspire any readers that are contemplating a veterinary career. It will give them some idea what veterinary life can be like and what is expected of a veterinarian. Maybe it will also give readers insight into the sometimes difficult and heartbreaking tasks veterinarians are faced with. I hope the different aspects of the book, some funny, some sad, will also be entertaining reading for anyone.

The events are true even if every detail may not be recalled exactly. The names have been changed. The events and people have been depicted as they appeared to me and the stories are never intended to harm or ridicule.

I thank all the people who trusted me to care for their pets. I always used to put my whole soul into my work and always put the welfare of the animal first.

1

Becoming a vet

After running a dairy farm for five years in New South Wales and a Santa Gertrudis cattle stud in South East Queensland for eight years, I decided it was time to go back to university. I studied in Stockholm in the seventies and have a science degree from Stockholm University. I was accepted into the University of Queensland as a mature age student to do the five-year full-time course, Bachelor of Veterinary Science.

I found accommodation in Brisbane with an elderly lady. I had my own entrance to a flat with a garage underneath. Every morning, I would drive to the university campus and park in their car park for the day. We had lectures and workshops from 9 am to 3 pm every day. I used to tape most of the lectures and go through the tape at night. On Friday evenings I drove up to the Santa Gertrudis stud I still worked on in my spare time. I also had my horses there. I used to muster cattle over the weekend and on Saturday night I would study. Sunday afternoons I drove back to Brisbane to start uni the next morning.

I loved every minute of the course. I was committed to getting through with good marks. At the end of each semester we had six to eight exams spaced a couple of days apart. I had not sat for exams for twenty years and not done so in this country, so I didn't know what to expect. It was totally different to the exams I had done at Stockholm Uni.

After the five years of hard work, I finally graduated as a veterinarian with honours in 1993. Now I could start my new career!

2

My first cow caesar – and in the dark!

MY FIRST JOB AS A very green vet was in Allora, a small country town in South East Queensland. It was a three-vet practice, and they handled a lot of cattle work. It was nothing to travel two hours to attend a cow. The countryside had a lot of cropping land as well as grazing for cattle. It was flat and uninteresting. There were some large feedlots for cattle. The summer temperatures could get very hot and the winters very cold.

Having worked with cattle extensively as a cattle stud manager for around 8 years, and spent 5 years managing a dairy with 70 cows that had to be milked twice a day, 7 days a week, 365 days a year, I wanted to further my experiences with cattle, this time as a vet.

I had had barely any practice at university, so now was the

time to learn how to actually do things. I found out that a lot of cattle owners worked in town and only saw their animals either very early in the morning or late in the afternoon. Or else they looked at them on Sundays. So those were the times they mostly called you.

Calvings were one of the most common reasons for contacting the vet. If you were lucky the animal had only been trying to calve for one day or less, but often the cow had been in labour for days and by now had given up trying and had a very smelly foetus either half out or still totally inside her. Unfortunately my first calving as a new vet happened at night.

It was a twenty-minute drive from the vet clinic to my friend's place, where I was staying. The phone rang just as I arrived home from a day in the vet clinic. A Mrs Smith was on the phone. She sounded distressed, saying that she had just arrived home from work to find her pet Guernsey cow with the two back legs of a calf sticking halfway out. Mrs Smith had tried to assist in the delivery but had hopelessly failed. She gave me directions to get to her farm, which I jotted down on a bit of scrap paper.

First I had to drive back to the vet clinic (which was situated in the opposite direction to Mrs Smith's farm) to pick up the vet vehicle with all the equipment possibly needed. Mrs Smith's farm was about an hour's drive from there. It was beginning to get dark, so I hurried a bit, but I knew it was futile to try to get there before dark.

After I turned off the main road onto a much narrower road, I picked up the piece of paper with the directions I had jotted down earlier. The cabin lights in the small, battered vet car refused to work, so I pulled up and got out into the car's headlights to try and decipher the note. It was winter and cold and had started to rain gently. The paper note with the directions got wet and soggy as I tried to read it. *If you come to Riley's Creek you have gone too far.* I got back in the car again and drove a few kilometres down the road. I looked for the *driveway on the left with the green cream can.* A white sign with "Riley's Creek" on it stared me in the face. I had gone too far. By now I was somewhat flustered, but I managed to make the decrepit old vet vehicle do a three-point turn on the narrow country road, hoping it wouldn't end up in the ditch. I then backtracked to the farm. At last I found the cream can on its side ready to receive its mail. I turned off the road and drove up the bumpy, rutted dirt track.

My apprehension by this stage produced huge butterflies in the depths of my stomach – by now very empty since I had not had anything to eat since midday. The rain had settled in, and the windscreen turned into a muddy blur. I managed to outline a building through the murk. Now where were the yards? I drove past the building that I presumed was Mrs Smith's house.

The yards were 200 metres further on. I pulled up as close to them as possible without getting stuck in the mud, so that I could carry the heavy equipment a lot more easily. (There were no four-wheel-drive cars at this clinic.) The air was cool, and it was going to get a lot cooler. It was pitch black to me, after looking into the beam of the car's headlights earlier. I felt my way to the yard and squeezed my body in between the round hand-hewn rails. I had just enough space to fit through. The lone golden Guernsey cow in the yard looked at me with sad, pain-filled eyes. She stood in the race with the two legs of her unborn calf sticking straight out from her vagina.

Mrs Smith was a weathered, middle-aged farm woman with a long ponytail down her back. She was dressed in jeans and a jacket.

"The calf won't shift; it is well and truly jammed. Poor old Daisy must have been trying to calve all day," she said with concern.

I went up to the cow's rear end to make sure that it was indeed the hind legs of the calf that were sticking out of the cow. I felt the hocks, which meant: hind legs. The soles of the calf's feet pointed upwards, indicating that at least the calf was not lying upside down. The calf was most certainly dead; it had drowned with its head still inside the uterus of its mother.

"We can try with the calf pullers," I said, "but first we'll have to tie the cow's head to the rails somewhere in the yard where there is lots of room in case she goes down."

I went to get the calf pullers and a rope. The rain had ceased, but the air was quite chilly. The ground was grass-covered, but the dirt was churned up into mud by cattle hooves.

Daisy was a sensible, quiet cow, so I could put the neck rope over her head and the two curled horns without too much difficulty. Tying her to a rail was a bit harder. Cows can be very stubborn indeed when it comes to putting them where you want them. I didn't want to give her too much rope in case she swung around at the end of the rope at the crucial time of fitting the calf pullers to her rear end.

I started to fasten the stainless steel calving chains around the calf's legs. The calf pullers looked like some barbaric instrument of torture from the Middle Ages. A two-metre-long, somewhat rusty steel bar with grooves along its entire length, and at one end a cross bar that fits across the cow's thighs below the protruding calf. The chains from the calf's feet hook on to a ratchet with a lever that moves the ratchet down the bar. When the chains are tightened, the operator pushes onto the bar towards the ground. This usually prompts the cow to strain simultaneously with the legs of the calf being pulled downwards. As the calf gradually appears, the chains may have to be reset higher on the calf's legs, otherwise one runs out of bar.

No amount of pulling and twisting of this calf could make it budge. Sometimes changing the angle at which the calf's hips are aligned or offsetting the chains so one leg comes out slightly before the other will allow for delivery, but this calf's hips were jammed at the pelvic brim of the cow. Daisy had gone down during the procedure and was lying flat on her side. The stress of the situation was mounting inside me.

"It looks like a caesarean," I said, trying to sound as calm as possible even though my guts were feeling more like a butter churn.

"She had a caesarean last year as well," Mrs Smith said unexpectedly.

I thought, *Why on earth keep a cow for a second round if she proved to have trouble last time?* She wasn't a little heifer last year even, and she was a roomy big cow now with a very narrow pelvic canal.

I nervously considered the approach I would use. This was my first caesarean section ever. I had never performed one on any type of animal or even seen one done, let alone in the dark. Luckily I had done a few post-mortems on cows, so I had a good idea of a cow's anatomy.

The most commonly used surgical approach is the left flank, either with the cow standing or sitting down. Since there was no crush available to put the cow in, it would have to be done with the cow sitting down on the ground. I just had to make sure she didn't go down on the wrong side. I went to the car to try and find the torch so I could get set up for the surgery. I asked Mrs Smith to get two buckets of clean warm water.

Because cattle are ruminants and regurgitate their food as part of their normal digestive processes, it is too risky to give them a general anaesthetic. If stomach content got into the lungs the cow would most certainly end up with pneumonia and die.

Back then a sedative became available that would nearly put them to sleep sitting up, and it also greatly reduced the cow's perception of pain. The sedative worked well on quiet animals but not so well on nervous or stirred-up cattle (as I found out later in my career).

I drew up the minuscule amount of sedative I considered needed for this already stressed cow. The easiest way to inject the substance intravenously is in the tail vein, because the tail is usually the most accessible part of a cow. Preferably the cow should be restrained during the procedure. Daisy had gotten to her feet and was wandering around in the dark yard – I had released her head tie earlier so she didn't choke when she went down.

Now I had to sneak up to her from behind, trying to grab her tail. I finally managed to get hold of the very end of it. There I was being dragged around by a cow's tail in the dark in a muddy yard, trying to find a tail vein for the first time in my life! She didn't want to cooperate at first, but somehow I managed to give her the injection by feel. I had no idea how much of it went into the right place and if it would work at all! I just had to wait and see and hope and pray!

After a few minutes Daisy started to stagger and finally sat down. *My gawd, something is working!* Luckily her left flank was exposed, so I didn't have to push the 400-kilogram cow over to her other side.

I started to shave the hair off around the intended incision site with a scalpel blade. Mrs Smith had meanwhile driven the tractor to the yard and left it running with the headlights on the cow. I had to squint not to get dazzled by the beam shining in the corner of my eyes. At least it was better than the torch. I asked Mrs Smith to position herself at Daisy's head and stabilise her so she didn't put her head on the ground, putting her at risk for regurgitation and inhalation pneumonia.

After I had shaved and scrubbed down Daisy's flank with antiseptics, I injected lots of local anaesthetic in an inverted L-shape to block out any pain associated with cutting the skin. The incision is made vertically just behind the ribs with a scalpel. You have to cut through the thick hide first and then the three muscle layers, being careful not to cut into the huge, bacteria-laden rumen (the second of the four stomachs of a cow), which lies directly under.

Because Daisy had had similar surgery the year before, her abdominal organs had become adhered to each other. I had difficulty passing my hand past the huge 200-litre rumen full of grass. I wasn't sure if I was in the right spot even, because I had to force my hand in to carefully break down the adhesions behind the rumen to reach the uterus with the calf. It took nearly the length of my arm. At least it was warm in there! I put a scalpel blade in my folded right hand, inserted the whole length of my arm again and started to blindly incise the uterus by feel, trying not to cut into the calf inside.

Now I had the task of removing the dead foetus or calf. It was a huge calf, and I was having difficulty getting a grip on it. There is a lot of very slimy fluid around a foetus to assist the cow passing it, but that also makes it very hard to get a grip on the calf. I was concerned not to open too big a hole in the cow. I decided to amputate one of the dead calf's back legs, which were still sticking out of the cow's vagina, with a special wire that acts as a saw. I inserted the wire via the flank incision, placed it by feel around one of the calf's legs, and started sawing. After the leg was removed, Mrs Smith and I both hauled and pulled upwards on the rest of the forty-five kilograms of stubborn and very slippery dead weight. After much sweating and struggling on our part, the lifeless body finally made its entry into the outside world via the artificial opening in Daisy's flank.

Daisy was none the worse. She must have felt relieved after getting rid of the obstruction in her pelvic canal. Now I had the compelling task of putting everything back together again! It must have been around ten o'clock at night. I was soaking wet from top to bottom from foetal fluids, blood, urine, faeces and rain, but didn't feel the cold yet because of the strenuous and very physical activity which is often part of the work.

I had to suture up the womb, or uterine horn, first. Ideally you are supposed to be able to pull the darn thing out in the open so you can put neat sutures in it before you put it back. I could not manipulate Daisy's womb in this way. It was adhered firmly to her inside. It looked as if I had to sew it up by feel inside the cow. There are a lot of touchy-feely jobs in veterinary!

After what seemed like ages, I was ready to close up the flank itself. My back was aching from stooping over the cow for hours. I had to suture up the three separate muscle layers into two layers with sutures that would dissolve later on. The somewhat tricky curved needles used by surgeons are held by a set of needle holders that are supposed to grip the needle firmly when squeezed and then let go when squeezed again. The ones I had to use held the needle OK but refused to let go of it unless squeezed firmly a number of times between each stitch. My hand started to go numb from all the excessive squeezing!

At last I was ready for the skin, using a material that doesn't dissolve by itself and has to be removed later on. The hide of a cow is very tough indeed, and it helps if you have a really sharp needle. For some reason this very essential and small piece of equipment seems to be the most abused and neglected of all instruments in a veterinarian's toolbox. Armed with a worn and battered needle that had already been through countless cowhides, I started to try and insert the uppermost stitch in the cow's flank. After a lot of persuasion, pushing and sweating, I managed to get the blunt needle through the hide. I had to place a continuous "blanket stitch" of the kind that is well known among sewing enthusiasts. It works very well to hold a cow together.

Daisy was now already eager to get to her feet and I was eager to pack up and go home. I gave her some antibiotics and some oxytocin to help the uterus contract. I told Mrs Smith to keep Daisy in the yard so she wouldn't get into trouble if fighting with her mates.

As I drove home sometime after midnight, I was soaked to the bone, thawing out with the car heaters fully on. This was an experience to remember.

I started work at the clinic again the next morning as usual at 9 am. Since this clinic was the first employment I had since graduation, I didn't expect much pay, and I never got paid extra for any after-hours work I did. I was so pleased with myself that I had managed to do what I did. I felt like I had achieved something. That was more worth than money.

Three months later Daisy was going fine, and her owner was fattening her up to be sold.

3

Midget the Chihuahua

A YOUNG LADY WITH SHORT DARK hair, Rosie, came into the clinic with a little black-and-tan Chihuahua named Midget, who did not look happy at all. Midget was eight years old and very friendly. He managed to wag his little tail, which must have been a great effort for him. He even licked my hands as I gave him a pat.

When I picked him up to the examination table his big sad eyes looked up at me as if to say *help me, I am feeling so terrible*. We already had a connection. I fell in love with him instantly. I had to find out what was going on with him so I could help him. The first important thing we do is to check the patient's body temperature. It was perfectly normal, which is always an encouraging sign. But poor Midget was very dehydrated and in very bad shape overall. I had no idea what was going on; I needed more information from Rose.

"How was Midget yesterday, did he eat anything?" I asked.

"We fed him some bones and he ate them with no hesitation," Rosie replied. When I heard that I thought that maybe he had a bone perforating his bowels.

Midget tried to stand on the examination table, but his legs seemed too weak, and they just folded under him. I informed Rose that I had to admit the little dog for further tests.

After Rose had left, I thought I could start by at least giving Midget an enema to get rid of some very dry faeces. When I was about to put Midget on an intravenous fluid drip which he badly needed, Rosie's' mother phoned.

"How much is all this going to cost?" she asked. "We don't have a lot of money and can't afford any more treatments. Rosie will come back and collect Midget later."

True enough, an hour later Rosie arrived with tears in her eyes. She paid the bill and picked up the sick little dog. They both left for good out the door. I wondered, what would happen to Midget now? I had already formed a connection with the little dog. I felt the pain as if I had let him down. Would they just let him suffer and die in agony?

I never found out what happened to the little Chihuahua. Did he recover or did he die in pain? Sometimes being a vet can be very disheartening.

4

The Blonde Vet

WHEN I WENT THROUGH UNIVERSITY I was divorced and a happy single girl. In the last year I decided to spruce myself up by bleaching my very short hair very blonde. This sometimes led to some flattering comments. I become known as the "blonde bombshell" at the university.

In the early nineties, when I was at uni, more than half of the veterinary students were female. This was contrary to a generation before, when the veterinary profession was nearly entirely male. I had never really noticed any public prejudice against female vets, not even when dealing with large animals. Only one funny incident comes to mind.

I was called out to attend a calving during business hours instead of the usual early morning ones when working at Allora in Queensland. It was a dairy cow that had tried to give birth to her calf back legs first. The farmer had tried to help the cow by pulling on the calf's legs but to no avail.

On arrival at the farm, I walked up towards the dairy. I was greeted by the farmer in the doorway of the building. The farmer then introduced me to his old dad, a frail, weathered man in his eighties.

"Are you the vet, eh?" the elderly gentleman asked with a shaky voice. He then continued, "It's bad enough when the vet is female, but when she's blonde as well it's even worse!"

I smiled and told the elderly man reassuringly that I was quite capable of assisting cows in labour. I could tell the old man didn't mean any harm – he just hadn't got used to the changes of the nineties. When he was young the women mainly stayed in the house, or if they had a job, it was mainly to do with secretarial or nursing-type duties.

The big red dairy cow had not been in labour long, but when the calf is coming back legs first there is a real danger of it suffocating or drowning if delivery is too protracted. I used the calf pullers that I described earlier as reminiscent of an instrument of torture, with the long metal bar with handles to winch the calf out by the legs. I removed the big bull calf speedily without much trouble. I instructed the farmer to hang the very slippery calf over a rail and rub it vigorously. It was a strong, healthy calf, and it soon started breathing with a few snorts and headshakes. After checking and medicating the cow I stayed for a while to make sure the calf was going to be alright.

On my way out the elderly gentleman stopped me with

a happy smile on his face. "I've changed my mind. I'll take back what I said earlier about female vets," he said. "I am very impressed. Thank you very much for coming out."

A "thank you" makes my job so much more worthwhile. I never forgot his nice remark.

5

The so-called "quiet" horse

EVEN WITH ALL THE YEARS of experience I personally have had handling horses of all kinds, dealing with them as a vet is a very different matter. You are not only dealing with the animal, but more so the people owning the horse. Traditionally, horse people are a breed unto themselves. They seem to have their own ideas about horse handling and care. And their horse and training methods are always better than anybody else's. As a vet you have to go along a bit with what the owner thinks is best for their horse.

In my very first week out as a practising vet I was called out to attend to a horse with a cut leg. My boss informed me the horse had apparently cut a V-shaped flap of skin on its front cannon just below the knee, and instructed me how this could be sutured easily. (I realise now that he couldn't have been told how large the skin flap actually was.) He advised me how much sedative a 500-kilogram horse would need.

"Give it six mils in the jugular and then a bit of local (local anaesthetic) in the leg and you shouldn't have any trouble," my boss told me. It sounded so easy.

I arrived at the property half an hour later, full of apprehension over my first horse stitch-up. A stern-looking man, with a woman I presumed was his wife next to him, stood on the lawn behind the house holding this big, fat, shiny red chestnut gelding with a white stripe down his nose. One front leg had a large skin flap hanging down below the horse's knee.

"Hi, I am Margareta the vet, I have come to see your horse," I introduced myself, trying to sound and feel as if I did this sort of thing all the time.

I opened the hatch door at the rear of the car to get a stethoscope and a thermometer. *I must give the horse a general check-up first*, I thought. As I walked over towards the patient, the big red horse nodded his head and pricked his ears. His nostrils flared as he gave out a loud snort. I halted my steps for a short while as the man holding the horse tried to settle him down.

"Whoa boy, whoa," he said, rubbing the gelding's face.

"You've got a beautiful animal there, Mr Reed. It's a nasty cut on his leg," I pointed out, trying to sound concerned. "When did he do it?"

"We saw him limping around this morning. Must have happened last night when we had that hailstorm. He's not too keen on things like that. I think he's hit the wire fence in the dark. Can you fix him?"

"It looks like a wire cut. I might be able to stitch it up." I tried to sound experienced, when in reality I felt terrified. "Is he quiet?" I asked, hoping the answer would be affirmative.

"Yes, yes very quiet," the man said.

"How old is he?"

"About ten as far as I can remember."

"Do you ride him at all?" I asked.

"Not for a few years. Don't get time anymore."

That could mean anything. Either he was not needed anymore, or he was too unreliable to ride. Who knew?

"It's a pity," I said. "He certainly looks like a fine riding horse. He is in such a good condition that he must be feeling above himself. A bit of work would make him less spooky."

While I was talking, I was carefully making the tense horse accept the touch of my hand on his neck. Every muscle in his body was on red alert, ready for flight. I wondered quietly how I would ever get a needle into this horse. For safety's sake I decided I had to sedate the horse before doing anything more.

"He's not too keen on strangers," Mr Reed said.

He's not too keen on a lot of things, I thought to myself. *Why do people put up with these mad horses when there are so many decent ones around these days?*

"I can put him in the cattle race," Mr Reed suggested. "We've had him in there before when we drenched him."

Personally, I consider races are meant for cattle. Horses are apt to injure themselves if restrained too much. I have seen horses rear up and hit their heads, or try to climb out and cut half their legs off in races. But in this case, I preferred the horse get hurt rather than myself.

The big horse behaved amazingly well in the race, which was situated in the shade under the roof of the farm shed. I clipped the side of the neck with scissors to see the vein better.

I then slowly injected six millilitres of the sedative xylazine into the big vein without much trouble. Some horses are very needle-shy and impossible to needle. Luckily this touchy gelding wasn't one of them! I instructed the man to remove the horse from the race into the yard before he got too sleepy. Soon he started to droop his head and look drowsy. Now was the time to try and examine the cut on the leg properly. There was a ten-centimetre flap of skin hanging lose beneath the horse's knee. I know now that such a large piece of skin was unlikely to grow back and should have been trimmed off, but the words of my boss, *can easily be stitched with a bit of local*, were ringing in my ears.

I slowly ran my right hand down the horse's front leg to the wound while whispering in a soothing voice, "steady boy, steady boy". I had to bend down to reach the horse's knee, which put my head in a more precarious place if he decided to jump away, or worse, jump on top of me. Lightning-fast, the horse jerked the leg away violently, nearly breaking one of my fingers. All of a sudden he was wide awake. My already-high heart rate doubled, and I felt like I was choking. I started to sweat with stress. He wouldn't let me touch the leg at all even after being sedated. I felt like a fool. I didn't know what to do next. I could sense the owner's critical eyes in my back. This sedative was worthless on this horse.

"I thought you said he was quiet?" I said shakily. "I need to be able to examine the wound."

"Yes, yes, maybe he doesn't like you," the man said with a snicker.

I decided I would phone back to the surgery for support. I felt a bit defeated, and this did not look good in the owner's eyes. *She doesn't know what she is doing!* My boss gave me the advice to "knock him out" with a general anaesthetic.

"I will have to give him a general," I said to the owner. I could feel how the man started to doubt my competence. With me being a mature person the expectations go up; they think you have done this lots of times before. But I had never given a sedative to a horse before, let alone an anaesthetic. We didn't get to do that at vet school. Most stuff we learned from blackboards and books. I knew that we had to use ketamine, but the horse needed to be thoroughly sedated beforehand, or they could go crazy … but that is another story!

This would be the first time I had "knocked a horse out" on my own, and I tried to steady my shaky hand as I injected the general anaesthetic into his jugular. After about half a minute the big chestnut started to sway, his legs buckled and he lay down on his side with a big sigh, fast asleep. So far so good.

I immediately started to attend to the injured leg, cleaning it with antiseptics. I then put some quick sutures in to attach the flap back to where it belonged. The horse kept waving the leg about the whole time, making the procedure most difficult. Halfway through, he started coming to life and struggled to sit up. I couldn't believe how soon he was coming to. The anaesthetic had only lasted a few minutes. It was supposed to last for half an hour. I told the man to sit on the horse's head to prevent him from sitting up, so I could finish the damned job. It was futile; how can you hold down a 500-kilogram horse that wants to get onto his feet? Before I had time to think what to do the horse was back on his feet with needles and sutures dangling off his leg. I felt desperately deflated. *What can I do now? I can't leave with half a job done!*

I was so embarrassed, but such is life. There is a first time for everybody. I decided to inform the now sneering man that I was just out of vet school and it was the first time I had had to stitch up a horse's leg. Of course, no one wants to see their animals used to practice on by a beginner. (My boss later told me off angrily for admitting to my inexperience. *You must tell everyone you have done lots before!* How does that work when you haven't?)

I had to ask the now impatient man if I could use his phone. There were no mobile phones then. I had to ask the boss what to do. I had to complete the job. My boss told me over the phone to wait twenty minutes and then give the gelding another dose of ketamine. Hopefully I would be able to finish the job then.

The gelding lay down nicely again after the ketamine injection as before. I finished off the suturing fast, holding my breath, and slapped a bandage over the whole thing, more to hide the awful job I had done than anything else. I managed just in time before the horse decided it was time to get off the ground again.

I drove home rather bewildered. Where did I go wrong? Why didn't the anaesthetic work long enough? The horse had been given the correct dose. And why wouldn't the horse lie still instead of waving his leg the whole time?

Two weeks later I found out that someone had to cut away the skin flap, since it wasn't viable and had dried up. I should have cut the flap away in the first place. Needless to say, the man never paid the bill.

I have since become a lot wiser regarding sedatives and anaesthetics in horses and now use combinations that work wonders on the most intractable equines. The problem is that when you work in someone else's clinic, you have to use what they have available there at the time. I have also learnt since that some equines are immune to the drugs I used, and they don't work at all no matter what the dose!

6

General horse behaviour

I USED TO LOVE HANDLING YOUNG horses when I lived in the country, and I rode horses every day looking after cattle. I absolutely adored horses in any shape or form. I could sit and watch them graze for hours. I learnt a lot about how they think by observing their social behaviour. It was clear that the younger a horse was, the lower its social status.

When it was time for them to come home for a drink at the water trough, all the horses wanted to get to the limited space at the trough at once. The older ones used to take their time sipping the water slowly. Then they would take a little snooze, standing at the trough without getting out of the way to let the younger ones drink. They seemed to enjoy teaching patience to their younger peers. The two-year-olds desperately tried to sneak up from behind and carefully stretched their necks out towards the surface of the water only to be savagely bitten by the older horses. The younger horses never learnt patience; they persisted in trying to drink at the same time as the others. They were always harshly chased away until their superiors had wandered off to graze.

This scenario was repeated every day. Then as the two-year-olds became three-year-olds they in turn kept the new two-year-olds at bay. It always fascinated me how the horses knew each other's age, but they were never wrong. The five-year-old would beat up the four-year-old who would beat up the three-year-old and so on.

Horses need their mates. They need a social hierarchy. They respect their leader and don't hold grudges like humans do. They work out their pecking order by biting and kicking. Once the order is established a mere snarl of the face with ears pinned flat against the neck will send panic among the inferior horses.

I had a four-year-old mare once. One day I introduced a small and stunted weanling into the same paddock, thinking they would both enjoy each other's company. But the mare took to the poor weanling with bared teeth and kept chasing it around the paddock incessantly. The weanling was pining for equine company and kept walking up to the mare. She saw the weanling as an annoyance and started galloping after it in big circles again. This went on for days but with less and less intensity. Horses cannot reason like we do that a poor and weak baby horse could do with a bit of gentle consideration instead of punishment!

I have also noticed situations where barren mares in a

group of mares and foals will protect a foal from potential danger. If a gelding in the mob walked up to inspect a foal, a particular "nanny" would storm up to the gelding with ears back and chase him off!

7

Caesar on a wild baldy cow on a Sunday

I WAS WORKING AT THE ALLORA clinic in South East Queensland. I was only doing two or three days a week, sometimes this included being on call for a weekend. In a three-vet surgery with a large cattle component, weekends were often quite busy. Farmers get up early and often check their cattle first thing. So they ring you early.

At 5 am this Sunday morning I was sound asleep when the phone rang.

"I've got a cow that can't calve," the voice on the other end said.

"What sort of a cow is it?" I asked.

"She is a big baldy," the man replied with a broad accent.

"Have you got a cattle crush?"

"Sure. If ya can get her in it."

"Why, is she wild?"

"Just a little. Took us two days to yard her when we realised she couldn't calve. Keeps charging at ya."

I was given directions how to get to the farm and left without any breakfast. I was too uptight to eat anyway. The sun was up, and it looked like it was going to be another hot Queensland day. First I had to pick up the car with the gear needed at the Allora clinic. I soon arrived at the farm, which wasn't far away. I spotted the big Hereford cow in a rather large set of yards. She was huge! There were three people walking about the place, two men and a woman. I pulled up next to the cattle crush.

"Isn't it a lovely morning!" I greeted the people to try and soothe my shaky nerves.

"She'll be a stinker I reckon," the man in an old Akubra hat answered as he walked towards me.

I walked over to the yard and climbed up on the rails to get a good distant view of the cow. She was a high-headed sort, too nervous to relax. There was no sign of a calf from her behind. She spotted me on the rails, scraped up the dirt with her front hoof, shook her head and started coming over in a threatening way.

"I need to examine her in the crush," I said to the man in the Akubra. "I don't know how we'll get her in there," I continued, trying to sound authoritative. "It would be foolish to get in the yard with her. The poor old thing is stressed to the eyeballs."

The two men started running about outside the yard yahooing and waving bits of polypipe around. The poor cow was stirring up clouds of dust as she tried to charge at them through the rails of the yard. After half an hour of this the cow was no closer to getting helped. The younger of the two men got into the yard. Since the cow wouldn't be driven maybe she would follow instead? The man waved his arms about to catch the cow's attention. After a few tries the confused animal finally ended up in the small forcing yard leading to the race and crush. The young man had speedily climbed the rails to safety.

Once in the crush I could safely examine the cow. Since nothing was showing from her birth canal, she might even be empty. Or it could be a total breech presentation with only the tail of the foetus facing entry into the world. I inserted my lubricated arm into the cow's uterus.

She had a calf in there alright. It must have been dead, because the cow smelt putrid. The dead calf was sitting on its haunches with the tail being the closest part of its anatomy that I could reach. Even with the entire length of my arm in the cow I didn't have a chance in the world to reach the back legs of the calf to try and pull it out by these first. It was a difficult breech presentation. There was no way I could correct the position of the dead calf, so I decided on a caesarean.

I injected the cow's tail vein with xylazine, usually a very effective sedative that makes most cattle, even the biggest and strongest bulls, want to lie down and forget about the world around them. After letting the cow out of the crush into the yard again, we all waited for the drug to take effect.

The big cow got more and more drowsy and staggered around but refused to sit down. I started to worry if she had received enough. Then I remembered a colleague telling me about a bull she had tried to sedate so she could treat it. The bull had been refusing to go down and my colleague told me she had been "running down the paddock after the damned bull stabbing it with a needle several times and it still wouldn't go down".

The sedative vets use in cattle is used instead of a general anaesthetic. But in some animals its effect can be overridden, especially if the animal has lots of adrenaline, which this cow certainly had. More of the drug does not necessarily mean more of the desired effect. On the contrary more can have the exact opposite effect, making the animal convulse instead.

Eventually the cow looked at the ground and sat down. I carefully crept up on her so as not to disturb her. But as soon as I got close, she managed to get to her feet again! I waited again until she sat down but the same thing happened. She got up as soon as I walked up close. This was starting to look embarrassing.

"We'll have to rope her to a rail and then tie her legs," I said to the people sitting on top of the rails looking on with amusement. I tried – with difficulty – to look experienced. I had never encountered this type of situation before in my life as a new vet.

I fetched a long rope with a noose at one end and managed to throw the noose over the poor cow's head. At least the sedative had slowed her down enough to be manageable. I then fed the other end of the rope over a sturdy-looking rail and asked the onlookers if they could try and push the cow closer to the rail so she wouldn't have so much rope to swing from.

The cow still refused to go down. I had given her a top-up dose of sedative, hoping it would help.

"We will have to throw her and tie her legs," I said. All 600 kilograms of crazy cow. I had a type of harness, called a sideline, that was used on horses to tie a back foot up towards the neck.

I started to put the leather neck straps around the cow's neck and the foot loop on her hind foot, while she was leaning back heavily on the rope around her neck as if paralysed. I slowly pulled her back leg up via the lever action of the sideline. The other three people simultaneously pushed on the cow and pulled on her tail to get her recumbent. Reluctantly she gave in and stopped resisting the ropes. I loosened the tie-rope around her neck to make her more comfortable but kept her still tied to the rails just in case.

The sun was now fairly high in the sky, and it was getting hotter. There wasn't any breeze. I was already exhausted and was sweating profusely. All the while I had an audience sitting on the fence around me. They seemed to enjoy the spectacle of a poor little female vet trying to subdue a huge dangerous cow. Nobody thought to offer the poor vet a drink of water in the heat that was now close to 30 degrees Celsius.

I managed to remove the huge, dead calf via a caesarean section on the cow's left flank. Halfway through stitching the wound up, the cow started to struggle violently and managed to just get to her feet regardless of all the ropes I had put around them earlier.

Darn animal, I thought. *You really don't want me to help you, do you.*

The cow stumbled and fell down again, this time managing to lie onto the open wound! Disasters of disasters! It is no easy task to roll over 600 kilograms of struggling cow. And now the open wound would be full of dirt. After eventually managing to turn the cow over to her right side, I wrapped her up with ropes from head to tail and also secured her feet to the bottom yard rail. I tried to clean the contaminated wound as best as I could and finished the surgery six hours after first arriving onto the property.

After being let go the cow immediately stood up and walked away. She looked no worse for wear. But looks can be deceiving. It had all been too much for her. She died later that day.

The man in the Akubra had contacted my boss and complained about the useless vet he had employed. He refused to pay the bill. Why did I do it? I think I wanted to prove to myself that I could do anything. I was very enthusiastic in the early days of my career and sometimes that backfired. I certainly had to learn the hard way. These days I am a bit wiser. I will not do surgery on an already distressed, wild cow, or if the calf is dead. The outcome is never good.

8

Breaking in a buck-jumper

I USED TO BREAK IN ALL my own horses. Mostly I bred my own, so they were handled from the first day and presented few problems. But sometimes I broke in a few horses for other people. These unknown prospects made me somewhat uneasy. There was one three-year-old thoroughbred gelding I will never forget.

The owner of the gelding considered him a friendly sort of a horse that used to come up to people in the paddock for a pat. The gelding was brown, and small and stocky for a thoroughbred. Anyone could walk up to him in the yard and catch him. He had been taught to lead and tie up but had never had a saddle on his back. The owner of the horse had an old round yard made of round bush timber and the yard was over two metres high. Many a horse had been broken in there.

I ran the gelding to be broken into the round yard and let

him settle for a moment before slowly walking up to him to catch him with a halter. He had a tense sort of stance and kept looking around at my hand when I touched him on the neck to get him used to me. He never made any attempt to move away, so I gently slipped the halter over his nose.

After he was caught, I spent some time getting him used to me by touching him all over his body and picking his legs up. He didn't seem to mind any of this, but he kept an eye on everything I did, which made me a bit nervous.

I used to lunge the horses in a halter only, so I decided to teach this horse to lunge in each direction. The round yard we were in was not on level ground, and the big wooden gate was in the downhill part. The horses often saw an opportunity to quit their training every time they went past the gate.

The brown gelding was a free-moving animal, and he was very willing to move out at the end of the lunge line. He went around anticlockwise with ease at a walk and trot. I decided it was time to go clockwise. This was an entirely different matter. Every time the horse came to the gate, he would turn his tail to me and spin around with lightning speed to try to go anticlockwise again. This is a common trait in lots of horses. They go easily one way but are totally stubborn when asked to go the opposite way.

This particular horse was extra-determined and very strong, and it took a lot to get him lunging properly. I decided to call it quits after one good run and let the horse out with his mates as a reward. I would work on him tomorrow again after he had had time to think about his lessons.

The next day I went through the same routine with the young horse. I got him lunging well and decided to get him used to a saddle while on the lunge line. I always used knee hobbles on all horses to get them used to standing still until asked to move off. Knee hobbles are made of a wide thick leather strap with metal squares that the strap can be fed trough. This is placed above the horse's knees between the front legs. Most horses would fight the hobbles the first time with a few awkward jumps but would soon decide it was easier to remain still.

The brown gelding had never made a fuss when first hobbled and stood quietly with hobbles on as I approached him with the old stock saddle from his near (left) side. He still insisted on suspiciously keeping an eye on everything I did. I carefully let him smell every part of the saddle so he could see it wasn't going to harm him.

When I was satisfied the horse had accepted the smell and look of the saddle, I slowly lifted the saddle over his back, being careful not to touch him with any part of it. I carefully lowered the saddle onto the blanket already in place on the gelding's back. Everything was well so far. No drama. With the help of a piece of wire with a hook at the far end, I ever-so-carefully got hold of the girth that was hanging down from the opposite side of the horse. I eased the girth underneath the horse's belly and lifted the saddle flap up to get to the girth strap on my side of the saddle. Then I gently threaded the girth buckle onto the strap and carefully levered the girth up hole by hole until the saddle was firm enough to stay on the horse. I very carefully bent down to release the knee hobbles and had only just got the buckle undone, when the horse moved forward one step. In an instant he must have become aware of the girth around his chest.

The brown gelding went off like dynamite that had just been ignited! He put his head down to the ground and lunged forward violently, lashing out with both hind legs high in the air. I still had hold of the lunge line and foolishly tried to pull the horse up. This only resulted in me getting in the way of his fiery backlashes. I got hit hard just below the ribs and fell to the ground doubled up with pain and unable to breathe. I thought I was going to suffocate.

Meanwhile the frightened horse was bucking and kicking madly around the round yard. I managed to crawl out of his way between the bottom rails. From this safe vantage point, I caught a glimpse of the mad buck-jumper going head first into a rail. The rail snapped in half and made way for the horse's body, which sailed through the air between the remaining rails. Saddle still in place, the furious animal landed on the other side still on his feet and continued his fight with the saddle in the next yard.

I had gotten my wind back but was still somewhat shocked by the incident. I had escaped without any serious injuries but decided to give this particular horse a miss.

The brown gelding proved to be a very girth-shy animal and bucked fiercely every time he was saddled. He eventually got broken in somehow. I don't know if he ever made it to the racetrack.

9

Talking to deaf ears

I HAD BEEN ASKED TO HOLD a talk on calving and calving difficulties (dystocia) in cattle at an agricultural school camp in Allora in Queensland. I spent a fair bit of time compiling a talk with drawings of different foetal positions, and I intended to bring along a few implements that were frequently used. A lot of the kids at the camp were from farms, so many of them would have seen cows and calvings before.

The talk was scheduled for 7:30 pm on Wednesday night. I worked as usual during the day at the Allora Vet Clinic. We normally finished the day by 5 pm, but this particular Wednesday I happened to be called upon to attend a calving just as it was time to go home for the day. So typical! This time it was a big Charolais cow that couldn't give birth to the calf because the head of the calf was bent back.

Charolais beef cattle are a French breed. They are

large-framed animals, tall and silvery white in colour. These particular traits were very helpful this evening, as the following story will tell.

When I arrived at my destination it was already dark. (Was this a conspiracy?) Luckily, calvings are mostly done by feel anyway. Only this time we ended up having to catch the darned animal as well, and in a feedlot full of mostly dark-coloured cattle. This is where the white coat colour came in handy. You could actually see which end of the mud-covered yard the uncooperative cow was heading for.

It all started simply enough: the tall, wide animal was actually presented to me in a race. The farmer had already had a go at trying to manipulate the calf inside the cow without any success. He informed me that the head of the calf was turned back which, when I investigated, was indeed true. There is no way a full-term calf can be born this way. I would have to pull the head back into the pelvic canal of the cow. This is easier said than done. It is very slippery indeed inside the uterus; this facilitates the birthing process, but it does nothing to help one to grab hold of bits of nose and ears. I found that putting a noose of a length of rope over a turned-back calf's head was the most successful way of securing the head and help bring it into its proper birthing position.

Now here is where the large frame of the cow came in handy. Normally I had to struggle with one hand and arm at a time trying to manipulate the noose over the slippery head. In this case *both* my arms fitted easily into the cow, which stood as tall as my shoulders. It was a song to slip the rope over the head of the unborn calf and to place its nose into the proper birthing position on top of the calf's forelegs.

The calf was still a tight fit, so the calf pullers were needed to get it out. To use these, we needed to get the cow out of the race and tie her to a rail in the open yard. To get her into a suitable yard we first had to run her through the feedlot full of steers! There was no other way. To be able to catch her in the big yard I had to put a very long rope around her neck before letting her go. So now she had ropes hanging from both her front and hind ends!

The big cow was no worse for wear and was full of beans when she was let go. She disappeared into the dark of the night and mingled with the fifty Hereford steers. With much coaxing and with people and cattle running everywhere in the mud, the cow was eventually drafted off into a separate yard by herself.

I now had the nearly impossible task of tying the long rope that was dragging behind her from around her neck to a rail. The rope kept getting tangled around her legs every time I got hold of it. Every time the cow got close enough to get the end of the rope around a rail, I tried to put as many throws around the rail as I could to try and hold the strong and stubborn animal. This can be a dangerous job as it is easy to get fingers caught under the rope. People have lost fingers this way.

The cow wasn't too impressed by being halter-broken at this time of her life. After a few tries we managed to stop her from throwing herself around. Instead, she now stood stubbornly, leaning back on the rope with all of her 600 kilograms, and was not going to budge.

With two men on her tail, pushing all they could, and me taking up the slack gradually, after a long struggle we finally got the cow into a position where she could be helped. The calf was soon delivered with the calf pullers. It was fit and well and the now recumbent cow soon got back onto her feet to care for her baby.

I didn't have any idea what time it was until I was ready to leave. Nearly seven thirty! It was at least half an hour's drive to the hall where I was going to hold the talk. I was soaking wet from foetal fluids, mud and blood and didn't have any change of clothing with me. At least it would be really authentic, with me arriving straight from a calving to hold a talk on the same!

On arrival at the hall I excused myself for being late, but explained that this was the true life of a vet. We never know where we will be one minute to the next. I was starving from having missed out on dinner again but got offered a cup of tea and a biscuit before the talk was to begin. I was eager to get the whole affair over and done with so I could go home and have a bath. Since I was late, they had already started, with another chap talking for what seemed like hours.

When it eventually came to my turn, the audience – which consisted of school kids – had lost interest. They were chatting and fidgeting among themselves. I might as well have talked to a wall. I felt terrible and wished I could finish the whole thing and go home. It was getting late. It must have been close to ten o'clock at night by then.

10

Marcia the draft horse

ONE OF THE SADDER INCIDENTS that happened to me as a vet involved a big bay Clydesdale mare. Her name was Marcia, and she was five years old. She was kept as a pet, but the owners had some plans on putting her in a cart at some stage.

I had been out on a difficult calving all Saturday afternoon. The phone rang just as I returned to the surgery.

"I have been phoning the surgery all afternoon. I always call your surgery. We don't use the other vet if we can get you." The woman on the phone had a French accent. She continued:

"I had the farrier to my dear Marcia to attend to her feet this morning. She is a Clydesdale and has huge feet. He trimmed her feet but had to use a sedative that the vets use because he couldn't get her to lift her feet up when asked. I don't think he is supposed to use a sedative, is he? She lay down after being sedated. After he was finished, she wouldn't get back on her feet. He tried everything but couldn't make her stand up. Then he seemed to want to leave in a hurry and mumbled something about something not being right with the mare. He said we ought to get the vet out to her as soon as possible. Then he packed up and left."

I was annoyed that farriers used veterinary drugs on their charges. It was against the law. A veterinarian would have to prescribe it to the farrier. A lay person had no idea what ill effects they could have on a horse. They did not have to go through five gruelling years to be licensed to use the dangerous sedatives veterinarians use. There was also something very wrong when an adult horse lay down after being sedated.

"I'll be out as soon as possible," I said.

I changed my dirty overalls to a clean pair and got the car organised for a horse call. From the vague information I had been given over the phone, I wasn't sure if the mare had colic (digestive trouble) or what could be wrong with her. The French-sounding lady didn't seem to know anything about horses. The mare seemed to have spent all her time unattended in a back paddock, so no one knew if she had been lying down before today or not.

It took over an hour's drive to get to the farm. The country looked glorious this time of year; we had had a lot of rain and everything was lush and green. The sun was just setting when I arrived.

It was a sad sight indeed to see this huge, beautiful animal flat on her side, obviously in a lot of pain. She showed no interest in getting up. I tried several times, coaxing her with a pull on the lead rope and calling to her. When I examined

Marcia her heart rate was over-the-top too fast. The insides of her lips were very yellow. She was jaundiced from not having eaten much for some time (Horses can get jaundiced from anorexia). There was a distinct bounding pulse in all four feet. The mare had an acute attack of laminitis, a crippling and very painful disease of the feet.

"Has anyone seen Marcia lying down for extended periods before today?" I asked.

One young girl, presumably the daughter, said she had seen the mare lie down on and off for maybe a week.

"Could she have gotten into a grain bin by any chance? Or any toxic plants?" I asked the owner. No, but it turned out she had been in a green paddock with some rye grass, and she also had access to some old hay that may have been mouldy.

I had to give the suffering mare a potent painkiller to help her. With a struggle we managed to get her onto her feet. She stood pathetically hunched up and with her hind legs under the body in a very unnatural stance, reminding me of circus animals trained to stand on a small table. She was quivering and sweating profusely with pain and had an anxious look on her big baldy face. I really felt deep empathy for this giant animal with her huge saucer-shaped feet. All that weight on four horrendously sore feet. Not even the painkiller seemed to have given her much relief.

I explained to Marcia's owner that laminitis was a disease of the feet that caused the bone of the foot to separate from the hoof wall, causing great pain. Laminitis was often caused by the horse eating too much lush feed or grain but could be caused by a number of things. It could cripple the horse for life. Treatment at best was mainly up to the farrier, who needed to fit special shoes to the hooves.

All I could do in this case was to instruct the mare's owner on a few things she could do that were quite labour-intensive, like soaking the hooves in hot water. (This is what I had learnt from the university lectures at the time, hot water not cold. Before this we had only used cold water.) They should bring the mare water to drink and hay so she didn't have to walk anywhere. It was better for the mare to lie down as long as she wasn't down for too long at once. I left some more anti-inflammatory painkillers to give to the mare in the next few days.

Ten days later the Clydesdale's owner rang me again. She had not been able to get a farrier to attend to Marcia's feet. She said the mare was lying down again and shaking. She had practically spent the whole ten days lying down. I was asked to come out for a revisit.

This time Marcia was standing up when I arrived. Her heart rate was a hundred beats per minute, an outrageous number – a horse's heart rate should normally be around or below forty at rest. The great mare was wavering from side to side trying to shift her weight from one painful foot to another.

I gave the mare an intravenous painkiller. It had been so long now with little or no improvement that I had to suggest euthanasia for the sake of the animal, which was suffering greatly. It seemed such a crying shame for such an outstandingly handsome young draft horse to have to be put down. Draft horses were far and few between at the time. The owner wanted to see if Marcia would improve in the next week, so I left her some more painkillers.

Nearly four weeks after I first had visited Marcia, her owner phoned me in great distress. She said Marcia was no better and they were going to have to destroy her. At least they didn't ask me to put Marcia down. A neighbour had shot her later that afternoon.

11

My first dog caesar: 2 am and the lights go out

THERE IS NOTHING LIKE LEARNING on the job. You never forget what you have done wrong! My first serious small animal incident happened well and truly at night at the country clinic in Allora. The clinic was conducted at the veterinary owner's home. He was on holiday at the time.

I was sound asleep at 2 am when the phone rang. The voice at the other end sounded decidedly distressed.

"My dog has been straining to have pups for half an hour and nothing is happening. She is really distressed, and we don't want to lose any of the pups. She's pedigree and we have people queuing up for her puppies."

I agreed to meet the owners at the surgery as soon as they could get there, which was in about an hour.

I quickly got dressed and drove the twenty minutes from my

friend's place, where I was staying, back to the clinic. I then put on the steriliser, which was a type of old-fashioned boiler, with the drapes and the instruments and went to phone the poor vet nurse, Amanda. Amanda lived across the road from the clinic and had worked there all her life. She was sound asleep but said she would be in directly. I was wide awake by now and started to scratch around for the anaesthetic that they normally used at this surgery. I was almost certain that I would perform a caesarean section on this bitch. Luckily Amanda knew where everything was and showed me the note with the dosage of anaesthetic. I was as ready for the big event as I would ever be.

"Here they are," Amanda whispered. "We usually let the owners stay during the surgery to help with rubbing the puppies as they are taken out."

I didn't like the idea of having the owners breathing over my neck at my first attempt at a caesarean. It would make me more nervous than I already was. Maybe it would be better if we sent them home? My mind was made up. I would send them home.

A very nice, rotund Staffordshire Bull Terrier arrived with its owners in tow – Mr and Mrs Preston. We all squeezed in to the minuscule surgery room, which also served as a consulting room. It had a small consult/surgery table in the middle and cupboards on the floor and on the walls. It had benches all around with sterilising equipment, an anaesthetic machine and other instruments, and a fridge. Bessie, the bitch, had not made any progress in producing a pup since I had talked to Mrs Preston on the phone. With a lot of difficulty, I lifted the heavy pregnant dog onto the stainless steel table.

I examined her carefully. She seemed fit enough. Her cervix was dilated, and I could only just feel a pup at the tip of my finger. Maybe her uterus or womb had become too tired to expel a pup. I decided to give her some oxytocin and calcium to see if that would make her produce a pup.

We all waited expectantly as Bessie started to strain again, but it was futile. Nothing was coming out. The recommended procedure at this clinic was to do a caesarean within an hour of the first sign of the bitch straining. I needed to be really well prepared to do a caesarean so the pups could be removed as quickly as possible before they got too much anaesthetic via the placenta. So I started to get Bessie ready for surgery by clipping the hair off her belly and scrub her skin. Bessie didn't seem to mind the slightest bit. Dogs are amazing creatures to just accept what happens to them. I hurt inside at her predicament. How could she be so stoic and just wag her tail?

I looked at the somewhat anxious owners.

"We will let you know the outcome as soon as it is over," I said to them. This gave Amanda the hint to see them out the door.

Now it was only Amanda and me. Amanda had a very nurturing and soothing nature. She gave me lots of confidence even though she herself wasn't a confident person. She had great faith in me.

"You are the vet; you can do it. Any vet can do a caesarean. We do one every week in this clinic. They just open them up on the belly and take all the puppies out and stitch everything together again. Then they send the whole lot home for the owner to worry about. There are never any problems."

Her trusting words gave me strength to tackle the task ahead. I had previously weighed Bessie on a set of very old bathroom scales that lived on the surgery floor, by holding her in my arms and subtracting my own weight. I wondered how many pups were hiding inside her. It was somewhat difficult to hold the dog and read the scales at the same time, especially as she wasn't particularly light, and not terribly cooperative with this weighing procedure. It would be disastrous if I dropped her onto the floor! But this was the way all dogs were weighed in this clinic. It was also a good way to keep a check on one's own weight in case it diminished out of sight from all the heavy work doing things like weighing dogs!

I finally managed to place Bessie on the stainless steel table and calculate the dose of anaesthetic needed. I had to try and inject the clear golden anaesthetic solution into a vein on one of the forelegs while Amanda held the leg. Good old Amanda! What would I have done without her? Bessie was very cooperative now and did not flinch at me penetrating her skin with the needle. The vein lies directly under the skin, and I had not had much experience at sticking needles into dogs' legs. If you miss there is no second chance, since blood will ooze out under the skin and flatten the vein. My hand was shaking with concentration. *What if I miss?* A small amount of blood flowed into the syringe and that told me that the needle was indeed in the vein. *I found it!* I slowly injected the golden liquid into Bessie's vein and her head started to droop as she fell asleep.

Now the second part of the anaesthetic procedure takes place. Amanda knew her job, having done this hundreds if not thousands of times before. She lifted up Bessie's head and opened her mouth wide so I could pull out her slippery tongue and visualise her windpipe. I now had only a short window of time before Bessie woke up again, to place a special tube into her windpipe. I connected the tube to the anaesthetic machine that would mix oxygen with the anaesthetic gas to keep Bessie asleep for the duration of the surgery. Amanda tied the tube to Bessie's jaw so it wouldn't come out. Now the real work could start! Scary! I always worry that the poor animal is going to die, and this time I think my heart rate hit 200 beats per minute. My hands were getting clammy with cold sweat.

We both positioned Bessie with her huge roly-poly puppy-full stomach on her back and tied her four legs to the table. Amanda scrubbed her shaved belly with antiseptic, and I had scrubbed up my hands meanwhile ready to open the sterile surgery pack. I covered the pregnant bitch with four large green sterile drapes held together with four clips. Now came the moment I dreaded most of all! I had to open her up!

I placed the sharp scalpel blade against her skin and started carefully cutting into it. Small amounts of blood oozed out along the incision. I needed a large hole to get the fragile uterus, huge with pups, out into the world without tearing it. I needed both hands to slip in behind the organ and managed to carefully exteriorise it onto the belly of the dog. It was enormous. A dog has a uterus with two long sections called "horns" that meet at the base. I had to incise at the base and then try to "milk" out the first pup.

My hands were shaking as I tried to grip the extremely slippery puppy. It looked strong and healthy. I handed it over to Amanda onto a dry towel so she could rub it vigorously to stimulate it to take its first breath. The next pup was harder to get to. I had to squeeze it along the narrow slippery horn of the womb as one squeezes on a tube of toothpaste. The pup then appeared at the opened part so I could retrieve it. I handed it to Amanda, who was now busy rubbing two pups at once. I could see how a lot of extra hands would help.

There were another two pups in the other horn that had to be sort of milked down to the outside world. Four pups in all, three boys and a girl. Lucky there weren't ten! Amanda got them all going and I could hear a soft whining from the cardboard box that Amanda was putting the pups in as they came to life. New life! What a delightful sound.

When I thought that I had found all the pups I realised that I had not pulled out all of the uterus; it was very tight in there and not easily done. I nearly missed the last one! It was hiding right at the furthest end. *Goodness me! What a disaster that could have been!* I never forget this moment and now I make sure that they are all out by pulling until the ovaries are visible.

Now I had the task of closing up the huge hole in Bessie's womb and abdomen. Catgut is used for all internal layers. It gets absorbed by the body after it has done its job. It is not made from cat's gut but from cattle intestines. Why it is called catgut I still don't know.

It was by now after 4 am and still pitch black outside. I was starting to feel a bit weary.

I had only started suturing up Bessie when all of a sudden, all the lights went out. Now it was pitch black inside the clinic as well as outside! This was disastrous.

"Can you find a torch or something?" I helplessly asked Amanda.

All I could do was to stand there with my blood-soaked hands on the dog, feeling its breathing rate. Thank God all the pups were out and well. Amanda came back with a weak torch and held it over the surgery site. It was very hard to see anything in the torchlight.

"That electric jug must have blown a fuse," I said to Amanda. "Do you know where the fuse box is? We may need some fuse wire also."

"I think there's a fuse box at the back of the building. I'll take the torch and go and check," Amanda said hesitantly.

I waited in the dark what seemed like hours. Then the lights came back on as suddenly as they went out. I cheered loudly. Amanda returned with a relieved smile on her face.

"I vaguely remembered something about an overload switch at the back of the house," she said. "I obviously found the right one."

"Fantastic," I cheered. "I got a bit worried for a while, but I knew you'd come up with something."

I finished suturing up Bessie's womb and abdomen, finishing off by closing the skin with a material that has to be removed after healing has taken place. Now all we had to do was to wait until mum recovered from the anaesthetic. She could then be reunited with her newborns. Ten minutes later Bessie was awake, and we put her into the box with her puppies. The pups were squirming about and soon started to look for the nipples for their first feed of milk.

It was 5 am as I drove back home to my friend's place, very weary. Luckily, I didn't have to work the rest of the day since I now only did two days per week at this clinic. I really felt sorry for poor Amanda though. She had to start work again in three and a half hours.

12

A hard choice: ethics or heroism?

At university we had very few practical hands-on sessions with cattle. Some were on privately owned dairy farms. We learnt how to pregnancy-test cows by first using the appropriate body parts from abattoirs. They had a model of a cow's pelvis that we could put our arms into and be shown how the uterus and ovaries were situated in the cow's body. In the living animal you obviously have to do the whole procedure by feel only. It takes a lot of skill and practice to distinguish the different organs inside a cow via the rectum and through the rectal wall.

First of all, your lubricated hand has to be gently but firmly pushed into the rectum. The cow usually strains at the same time and defecates profusely. The muscle that closes the rectum is very strong and can cause a lot of pressure on your arm, so your arm can sometimes go numb. Sometimes you have to scoop out the faeces manually to be able to feel anything through the rectal wall. Your entire arm needs to be inserted to be able to reach everything in a large cow. Often when a cow has had enough of being palpated, she strains so much that the entire rectum forms a stiff balloon, making it impossible to feel anything.

Farmers want to know if their cows are pregnant so they don't have to feed a cow for an entire year without getting a calf out of her. Good healthy cows should have a calf every year. To be as profitable as possible they should go into calf when they first come into heat, or *oestrus*, or at least the second time around about three weeks later. They normally cycle every three weeks. Cows are pregnant for about nine months.

Some farmers want to know as early as possible if their cows are pregnant or not. It takes a lot of skill to detect an early pregnancy by feel, since all there is to feel early on is an orange-sized swelling in one of the two horns of the uterus – two narrow extensions on the uterus or womb that many animals have in contrast to humans. One of these horns will contain the developing foetus.

On my first week out in the real world after university I was sent out to pregnancy-test forty head of cattle. They were all supposed to be early pregnant, and the owner wanted to know which ones were so he could sell the ones that weren't. My heart nearly stopped at the thought. Forty head! And early pregnant at that! I hadn't had *any* experience since the few cows I had felt at the practicals at uni.

As I reached my destination I drove up as close as possible to the race that already had all the cows packed in it, one nearly on top of the other. Cows don't like being packed in and restrained in a race, so some of them tried to climb on top of the one in front, or some tried to turn around and face the opposite way. Sometimes they got stuck with the head turned back the wrong way. The farmer told me that he wanted them done quickly because he had business to do in town.

The only way I had done this before was one cow at a time restrained in a head bail. There was no time for this to be done here; the farmer wanted it done fast! How some vets do this is by climbing over the top of the race and squeezing in between the distressed animals while being jumped on and pushed around. Or if your arm is long enough you can slip it in between the rails and try to reach each rectum!

I needed more time and care to be able to feel anything. I tried getting in between the animals but I am only small and light, and it was scary. There were horned heads everywhere, and they weren't happy. Needless to say, I had no hope of getting anywhere. I could sense the owner's irritation at having been sent an incompetent vet. I could not make out which cow was pregnant and which one wasn't. I felt so defeated. I had to phone the boss from the Allora Vet Clinic. He soon came out and did the whole lot in no time by the arm-between-rails method.

The expectations put on new vets were unreasonable. We were expected to know how to do everything firsthand. There were no apprenticeships for vets.

Afterwards my boss told me not to ever inform the client that a cow is *not* pregnant. Just say she is not detectably pregnant. If you say she is not pregnant and she then has a calf it will make you look stupid or incompetent. But if you say she *is* pregnant, and she doesn't have a calf, she could just as well have lost it later on! I wondered afterwards if he just informed the farmer that they were all pregnant anyway, why not? Should I have done the same?

Later on in my career I had much easier pregnancy-testing jobs to do, with only a few cows that were restrained one by one, and mostly much later in calf. With lots of practice the human brain learns to form a mental picture of what the fingers are feeling. It is like a sighted person trying to decipher blind text or Braille. A blind person's brain has learnt how to "see" the text by lots of training in feeling the dots with their fingers.

13

Feedlot steers in trouble

In southern Queensland, feed-lotting of cattle was getting quite popular when I worked as a vet. Cattle, mostly steers (castrated young bulls), are brought in off grass and put on a ration of different grains or concentrates. This has to be introduced gradually over some weeks. Cattle are ruminants, with four stomachs, and the food is chewed twice. The real digestion is done by microbes in the first two stomachs. There are numerous types of microbes, from bacteria to single-cell organisms or protozoa, that all have different functions and produce different by-products. The microbes also prefer different substrates, and the type of fauna that develops depends on what the steers are being fed. The worst that can happen is that a large amount of acid develops in the first two stomachs. This part of the cattle anatomy is not made to handle acid. The animal can get very ill and often dies as a result.

Another ailment that can occur when ruminants are on lots of grain are stones that can form in the bladder. They can get lodged on their way out when the animal tries to urinate.

I was called out one morning to a large feedlot with many hundreds of cattle. The manager, a weathered man in his fifties, had a steer already in the race for me to examine.

"I think he's suffering from water-belly," the manager said. "He's all hunched up and I haven't seen him pass urine at all today."

The poor animal looked terribly uncomfortable, and his belly was very swollen underneath.

"I'll have to do a rectal exam on him" I said. "That will soon tell if his bladder is enlarged."

When I passed my arm carefully into the steer's rectum, I could feel the enormously distended bladder. It felt like a football in there.

"The bladder is enormous," I reported. "At least it hasn't burst yet, then he would be history."

I remember when I was doing practical work during the vet course, I had been out with the practising vet to a similar feedlot case. The stone that blocks the urine flow is generally stuck further down towards the penis where the urethra is narrower. A salvage procedure to relieve the blockage is to cut a slit in the urethra where it emerges just below the anus. It traverses the bones just under the skin and is easily felt.

"I am going to make him into a female to bypass the stone," I said with a slight smile on my face. "He will pass urine through a surgical hole until he can be sold."

After cleaning the area, I cut a slit in the skin below the tail and then into the urethra underneath. A small amount of urine spurted out. I needed a catheter to insert into the bladder to overcome the spasm that prevented the bladder from emptying. The veterinary vehicle had a lot of stuff in it but not everything. There was no catheter to be found.

"I need a catheter to insert into the hole I just made," I said to the manager, "but it doesn't look as if there is one in this vehicle. Have you got some tubing from an old vaccine pack? And a bit of stiff wire please."

The manager went over to a shed nearby and soon came back with some thin clear plastic tubing and some thick fencing wire. I cut the tubing to the length I needed and inserted the wire into it. Then I passed the tube with the wire inside it straight into the hole I had made. Carefully I passed the tube inch by inch into the urethra of the steer. I was trying to feel the resistance of the bladder in spasm. Finally I got to the bursting full bladder. A spurt of urine suddenly appeared from the end of the tube! It was a terrific feeling on my part, let alone what the animal must have felt. The flow of urine seemed to never end. The poor steer gave up a deep sigh of relief. This was one of the most satisfying moments in my career. I could sense the gratitude of this steer just by looking at his face.

I had basically turned him into a female as far as passing urine goes, with the urine coming out just below the tail like on a female.

A week later, I phoned the manager to see how the steer was doing. "He is doing really well, eating and passing urine well and will soon be ready for sale," I was told.

***

Feedlot steers in trouble

About two weeks later I got a call from this same feedlot manager.

"I thought I would call you out again since you did such a good job last time," he said. My head started to swell with pride!

"What have you got this time?" I asked confidently.

"One of the steers is down on the ground and he doesn't look too crash hot," he told me.

"Is he sitting down or is he flat on his side?" I asked.

"The steer is flat out with head on the ground and won't get up."

"I will be out directly."

I met the manager at the entrance of the feedlot, and he took me over to the downer steer. He was a Hereford-cross animal, only quite small, and he was clearly in a fair bit of pain. His eyes were in an unnatural position, with the white showing, and he was frothing at the mouth. He had profuse diarrhoea and was very dehydrated.

"How long since he was introduced to the concentrate ration?" I enquired.

"Only about a week."

"It looks like grain poisoning or acidosis," I explained. "It is very serious when they get to this downer stage. I don't hold much hope for him."

"Is there nothing we can try?" the manager asked.

"The only thing would be to open him up in the left flank and go into the rumen and empty out all the grain. They get a total stasis or standstill of the digestive system, and everything just sits there and ferments and rots and lots of acid is produced. His chances of surviving surgery here in the open are slim. By rights he should be on a drip in an intensive care ward."

"Let's give it a go anyway," the manager said.

I had done this before on dairy cows that are still standing and well. But never on a case like this. The full rumen on a big cow contains up to two hundred litres of ingesta (feed). It is a huge job to empty this out by hand via a small hole in the side. But this little steer shouldn't be so bad.

I fetched my surgery gear and started shaving and scrubbing up the left flank on the steer. I had given him a minute amount of surgery-type sedation first. I injected a local anaesthetic around the area where I had to cut him open. I then incised the skin and the underlying muscle with my scalpel. Carefully I cut an entry into the rumen, trying not to spill any of the ingesta into the abdomen; that would be disastrous. Then I had to suture the edges of the rumen to the skin so it formed a tight seal.

Now the fun began. With my bare hands I scooped out the rotting, acid-smelling grain until there was nothing left. The steer was still alive but only just. All I had to do now was to stitch up the rumen and then the muscle and the skin. The manager thanked me, and I went on my way.

The next day I found out the steer had died that afternoon. It wasn't unexpected. And you can't win them all.

14

On call all night

I WAS DOING TWO DAYS A week at the Allora Vet Clinic. For several months I drove up the day before from Brisbane and stayed with a friend on a farm. Later on in the year I stayed with the other vet who was employed in the clinic. She and her partner rented a house in Allora itself so it was close to go to work. I stayed in a spare room and slept on a foam mattress on the floor that I had brought up with me. In those days when I was on call, I had a somewhat bulky mobile phone on the floor next to my mattress. At the end of my shift, I used to drive back to Brisbane in the evening after the two days' work.

Sometimes I had calls really early. Farmers would phone at 4:30 am and ask some questions about something that had just happened to them. I found it very hard wrestling my brain for information as I had just been woken up from a deep sleep.

One night a woman called me at 2 am.

"Allora Vet Clinic, Margareta here," I answered with difficulty.

"My dog is in so much pain," a woman sobbed at the other end. "I don't know what to do."

"Can't you bring him into the clinic?" I asked, a bit bewildered.

"I live three hours' drive from you. Dr Smith does a weekly run past my place. He told me Butch has inoperable cancer. He is in so much pain I just wondered if there is something I can do to help him."

It is always difficult for me to know what to say or do in these situations where the patient has been treated by another vet and I don't have a clue what's really going on. I have never seen the animal and have not got any records next to my bed to look up in the middle of the night. All I can go by is what the owner tells me.

"All you can do is keep him warm and comfortable and talk to him. I am sorry, I can't really help you anymore." I felt awful that I could not do anything more.

I tried to go back to sleep but found it hard when thinking about the owner of Butch and what she must be going through. Finally I went back to sleep, only to get woken up again by the phone.

"I am phoning about Butch again. I feel so helpless that I can't ease his suffering. There must be *something* I can do!"

I basically repeated what I had said the previous time. It was now about 2:30 am. When I finally went back to sleep again the phone rang for the third time. It was Butch's owner again. This time I started to feel annoyed and also helpless. I could only try and comfort the owner by being at the other end of the line and sympathising with her agony.

In the morning we had consultations as usual, starting at 8:30 am. I had to drag myself in to the clinic. The vet nurse knew Butch and his owner. She told me that Butch, sadly, had passed away that morning.

15

Ungrateful farmers

As I only worked for two days a week in Allora, I had to be on call those two days, including up to 8 am the last morning when I was due to go back home to Brisbane. This was such a morning; I had a call at 7 am. It was from a farmer.

"I have a cow down. She's due to calve any day, but there is no sign of a calf or anything," the farmer said.

"OK, I will be right out." I knew very well that I would probably be there for hours. I didn't get any extra pay for doing after-hours calls either. It was all in the learning.

On arrival I was shown to a nice Jersey cow that was sitting down on the ground. After examining her rectally by lying flat on my belly, I concluded that she was in early labour. Her cervix, the entry into the uterus or womb, was only half open and she wasn't pushing or straining at all. After a full examination including listening to her heart with my stethoscope, I suspected she had milk fever. Milk fever is common directly *after* calving but less common just before or during calving. It is caused by a sudden decrease in blood calcium, since a lot of calcium goes into the milk. Without calcium the muscles in the body won't work. The cow was basically paralysed and unable to push the calf out or stand up.

"She has milk fever, and I will give her some calcium straight into her veins," I informed the farmer.

I went down flat on my belly again and tried to manipulate the calf, but I failed miserably. The tight half-opened cervix prevented the calf from fitting through.

My boss had told me that in cases like this, farmers want results, so it would be best to do a caesarean section on the cow to get the calf out if it couldn't be born naturally.

"I will have to do a caesarean," I told the farmer.

He informed me that he had to go into town on business.

Typical, I thought, *leave me here with this huge job.* I relied on people helping with bringing buckets of warm water and with a bit of muscle in case it was needed. I felt really dismayed.

After the farmer left, I started doing the surgery to remove the calf. I struggled to lift out the slippery forty-five-kilogram calf through the surgical opening without any help. And sadly, the calf had just died from the stress of being unborn for too long. It was not getting sufficient blood supply to the placenta from a milk-fevered cow. I stitched the cow up and left her sitting there with the dead calf next to her. It was now 10 am and I was keen to get back to Brisbane. I would not be paid any extra for these hard hours.

Next week when I was due for another two-day shift, the boss told me that the owner of the cow had phoned back and complained that the calf was dead, and he was not going to pay the bill. I could not believe it. Some people are always looking for a reason not to pay for the work we do. Such is a vet's life!

16

The blue-stained overalls

Cattle are not as robust as they look. Their intricate digestive system leaves them vulnerable to a lot of problems. The plant matter they eat can be fine one day and deadly the next. The most common and sometimes disastrous condition is bloat. Bloat is a sudden accumulation of gas in the first stomach of the cow, and it can get so severe that the animal cannot breathe because of pressure build-up in the chest. Dairy cows are sometimes grazed on lucerne because it is very nutritious and high in protein. Unfortunately, it is also prone to producing bloat. For a multitude of reasons some cows will suddenly fill up with gas when grazing lucerne or other legumes. They can die rapidly from suffocation if nothing is done.

On one occasion my boss was out to a dairy farm with a herd of beautiful and valuable Friesian dairy cows. Several cows had gone down and died over a couple days. This was a real emergency. My boss rang me and asked me to come out to help. It was getting dark (seems to be the common theme!) so the farmer left all the lights on so I could find the place in the dark. It was a fair drive to get there.

There were a couple of cows that had gone down that were still alive. The presumptive diagnosis was nitrate poisoning, not bloat this time. This can happen after a dry spell when rain makes the pasture grow again. The plants can then accumulate more nitrate than normal. The cow's digestive system can't handle too much of a toxic breakdown product of the nitrate. When the excess amount gets into the blood stream it binds to the haemoglobin in the red blood cells; this prevents the blood from taking up oxygen, and the cow dies from oxygen starvation of the whole body. It is a very cruel and painful death.

The strange treatment for nitrate poisoning was to inject methylene blue into the jugular vein! This is a VERY blue dye. I had to inject several cows with this dye in the dark to try and save some of them. Needless to say, a fair bit went onto my overalls as well as into the cows.

The next morning, we both went back to try and figure out what was going on. There were dead cows everywhere, more like a war zone than a farm.

"Why don't we test the drinking water for nitrate?" I suggested to my boss.

"You bloody bitch, don't tell me what I should do!" he replied. He was very stressed and bewildered and said something nobody should hear. The farmers wife overheard the rude reply.

"Don't take any notice of him," she said, trying to make me feel better. "You have both done a great job in a very stressful and impossible situation."

We never found out what caused the tragic and immense losses of stock the farm experienced. I still have a lifelong memory of the event in the form of very blue-stained overalls.

17

Port Hedland Vet Surgery: A hard kind of job

WHEN I GRADUATED FROM THE University of Queensland, I decided that I wanted to see Australia and get experience by working out in the bush as a locum. So when a locum position became available in February in the north of Western Australia, I jumped at the opportunity to see this part of the world. My prospective employer would pay for the return airfare.

After a long and tiring flight from Brisbane via Perth, I arrived 3 pm in Port Hedland, a mining town right on the north-western seaboard. On the approach to the airport, I could see the beautiful white trunks of the river gums lining the dried-up riverbeds. Their green, hanging foliage contrasted strongly with the red dirt.

In this part of Australia the desert meets the sea. The daytime temperature used to reach 40 degrees Celsius for much of the year and the air had around 90 per cent humidity. If it had been a dry heat, life would have been that much more liveable. The maximum change in high and low tide was an amazing seven metres. When the tide was out there was bare sand banks as far out as you could see. At specific times the moon would reflect in the many puddles at low tide to create an effect of a luminous vertical ladder, the "staircase to the moon", leading up to the moon itself.

I was picked up at the airport by the managing vet, Dianne, and her vet nurse, Michelle. It was a Wednesday afternoon, and they were normally free of consults. I was to stay in Dianne's house, next to the surgery, for the month I was intending to work there.

Port Hedland has a sister town, South Hedland, that lies a fair way inland. The ground around Port Hedland is very low and is inundated with salt marshes from the tidal flow. The town ran out of room to build on so South Hedland was founded. To get from one to the other you have to cross the iron ore railway. If you are unlucky you may have to wait half an hour or so while the immensely long iron ore train crosses the road.

South Hedland vet surgery was where we were heading. Port Hedland itself did not have a vet at all, which was going to be all too apparent. The surgery was situated next to the sewerage works of all things. Dianne's house had a spacious yard full of big trees. The whole lot had a very high solid board fence around it. It appeared more like a fortress. In the yard two shaggy, growling wolfhounds roamed at will. The ground consisted of deep sand, hot and dry.

Apparently the town wasn't a very friendly Australian town. Alcohol abuse among the locals was a big problem. This was only too obvious around the shopping centre, where groups of First Nations people were seated on the grass all day every day drinking alcohol. Even inside the air-conditioned shopping centre there were often intoxicated people wandering around aimlessly and shouting at you as you walked past them. The usual supermarkets were rather dirty compared to Australian standards. They kept open twenty-four hours a day because of all the shift workers in this town. And the price of food was accordingly very expensive.

I wondered what single female wanted to run a vet surgery in this place. You'd have to be tough. And the heat was almost unbearable! All the houses in this town had air conditioning. You couldn't live here without it. But it cost a small fortune to run it, especially in some houses made of corrugated iron without any insulation. I saw some very unusual houses indeed. More like shanties. The visitors to Port Hedland described the town as "unloved" in the tourist bureau's visitor's book. One thing I noted was that bougainvillea plants absolutely loved the place – there were huge, beautiful bushes in the town full of gorgeous red flowers. This made a big difference to the otherwise grey and dirty look.

Dianne's three-bedroom house was old and dilapidated. I was to sleep on a simple single bed in a bedroom full of junk. The house had air conditioning, but Dianne never put it on, so the nights were most uncomfortable. I slept with nothing on and only had an ancient small fan which I, with difficulty, tried to direct towards the bed. My skin constantly felt sticky. Dianne's bedroom was at the end of a hallway, and she kept her pet kangaroo in it all the time. The two big wolfhounds, plus another smaller dog, also lived in the house some of the time. Needless to say, the carpet and the furniture weren't exactly clean, especially as the two big dogs constantly drooled saliva everywhere.

On the other hand, the vet surgery had been given a recent face lift and was very spacious and modern, with several remotely controlled air conditioners. It had a large waiting room, two small consulting rooms, a very large surgery area with two surgery tables and a huge animal room with lots of walk-in cages.

Dianne, the managing vet, was only in her early thirties and was obsessed with veterinary science. She was a very accomplished vet. She never seemed at ease and always had a stern look on her face. I felt sorry for her, since I could sense she wasn't a happy person. I soon found out that she was a workaholic and a perfectionist in the utmost sense. She had to be a workaholic to run this place; it had enough work to employ three vets full time. Luckily there were people in the town with nothing to do, so they helped voluntarily in the clinic with cleaning and so on. Dianne had been running the surgery for a couple of years, mostly on her own because she proved to be rather difficult to get on with.

She rarely left the surgery before midnight, and sometimes she was performing surgery until 2 am. She saw herself as some sort of martyr. Once she blamed me for her long day when I left the surgery at 11 pm because I was exhausted, attacking me the next morning with "I was up to 2 am to do that last case because you didn't do it."

If she hadn't had this obsession with her work she could

have treated some of the animals conservatively, which would have saved a lot of time.

One example that I remember vividly was a blue heeler that had been in a dog fight several days earlier. We saw a lot of similar cases. The dog had an extensive skin deficit on its forearm that had started to granulate (heal) nicely. Apart from skin grafting there wasn't much that could be done. But Dianne saw the need for extensive surgery under general anaesthetic. She spent at least two hours tediously scraping and flushing the dried serum off the dog's leg. It was getting close to 11 pm, but Dianne saw no need to try and cut down on the tedious scraping of the old wound. She had eventually finished off around midnight by putting two totally unnecessary little drains at the edge of the open wound. The next day the leg looked the same as before the two hours' surgery treatment.

I had been informed at the start by the owner of the clinic, who lived elsewhere, about the hours at the surgery, and there was no mention about regular midnight surgery. This was an absurd working schedule. No mortal person could keep this pace up for long. Consultation hours ran from nine in the morning to midday and then from three to six in the afternoon with surgery in between. To top it off I was ordered to pick up horse manure in the yard in the middle of the day in 40-degree heat. I felt like a slave from day one!

The clinic did not run on appointments. It was first come first served. Most clients arrived at nine with their pets, and the waiting room used to get pretty full every day. My job was to do the consults, which I enjoyed immensely.

18

Ticks galore

Every part of the world has its own veterinary peculiarity. In this part of northern Australia, it was the dog tick. I could never have imagined the extent of the problem. Fleas are normally the most important external parasite of dogs but here it was ticks! Millions of them.

Dogs used to come into the South Hedland surgery covered in ticks. Or they had them inside their ears nearly blocking the dog's external ear canal. Often the ticks were the reason the dog was brought in to the vet.

The ticks were scientifically known as the Brown Dog Tick. They ranged in size from one millimetre to ten. I had to advise the dog owners how best to treat the dog and prevent it picking up more ticks. The dogs seemed to pick up seed (baby) ticks in their own back yards where they lived, which mostly had a sandy soil. A heavy infestation could render the dogs anaemic and cause ill thrift. The ticks were also carriers of blood-borne dog diseases. When dogs had to be admitted to the hospital for any reason we always had to spray them all over first; otherwise the floors and walls would soon be covered with crawling ticks of all sizes.

19

The fainting client

When doing consultations at South Hedland Vet Clinic I had to judge whether to admit an animal for certain procedures or save time and treat the animal during the consult. This latter choice can have its problems and upheavals.

One hot usual afternoon I saw a happy little bull terrier with both its owners, a young couple. The man was a very tall, skinny person. The dog had a somewhat sore toe with a small abscess. I considered it unnecessary to admit the dog for such a minor problem and decided to incise the abscess and drain it on the consult table with the owners holding the dog. The clinic was seriously understaffed. This would save a lot of valuable time and make use of the owners as handlers. They both agreed to this as the best way.

I started cleaning the happy dog's toe with antiseptic. Holding the toe firmly in one hand, I made a quick stab into the tiny abscess with a pointed scalpel blade in the other hand. The dog didn't even flinch. A small amount of blood was oozing out from the toe onto the table. Suddenly I heard the tall fellow let out a faint drawn out wailing *aaaaah* as his legs gave way, and with a thud he hit the hard concrete floor. He had fainted from the sight of the blood from his dog! He was lying unconscious on his back. His girlfriend looked totally confused as whether to keep holding the dog or worry about her boyfriend on the floor. I was still holding on to the dog's bleeding foot and was in the same state of confusion.

I finally, after what seemed minutes, thought *stuff the dog, this guy needs attention more than his dog*. I let go of the dog, which immediately jumped off the table and ran off out the door as I opened it to call for help. It was leaving bloody footprints all over the floor as it went. The girlfriend seemed to have gone into a state of shock and stood staring with glazed eyes at the man on the floor.

"Can somebody help? A man has fainted!" I called out.

Dianne, the manager, didn't seem to take any notice whatsoever, but a girl who was visiting came to assistance and turned the man – still out to it – onto his side so he could breathe easier. After a couple of minutes he started to return to consciousness and sat up looking a bit bewildered.

Everyone had forgotten about the dog. It had gone for an inspection round the clinic, and there were bloody dog footprints everywhere. It had to return home without a bandage on its foot. The man was sent to hospital to be checked for concussion.

Ever since that incident I always ask people carefully if they mind blood or needles before I let them be present at treatments of their pets.

20

Port Hedland Tourist Bureau: An oasis in Hell

Port Hedland was a deserted-looking town. The weeds were growing tall in the main street. All the buildings were covered in red iron ore dust. The heat and humidity were so draining you tended to look for refuge in any air-conditioned place you could find, and there weren't that many.

Despite this, and although it was just a small mining town, Port Hedland still had a wonderful tourist bureau. It was a saviour to me as well as to many people before me. This oasis in a very inhospitable part of Australia was visited by many people from all over the world. People driving their own cars, and tour buses, all stopped outside this very well-run little shop. The outdoor temperature had been around 40 degrees centigrade every day during my stay in this neglected town.

Inside the shop it was nicely air conditioned. Extracts from the visitors' book:

"Unloved town, fantastic tourist bureau."
"Very hot! But terrific in here."
"Very hot, but extraordinary guy running this show."
"Best tourist bureau ever been to, ten out of ten!"
"Thanks Ted, you're a great guy."

Not only were the premises nicely decked out with lots of colourful souvenirs and local gemstones; the shop also had a lot of Australian books and a large television set showing videos from the area. There were lots of chairs to sit and watch the videos from, and a big table to do your own thing at. Numerous colourful and informative brochures were presented nicely along the walls. They tempted the traveller with information on the many awesome places to visit in the region.

Even the outside of the shop was well tended to. It had, among other plants, a lush green bougainvillea covered in gorgeous purple flowers. This species of flowering plant thrived in this hot and dry climate. The town had some spectacular specimens in a lot of places, and they really stood out in this drab environment.

What made this place extra special, though, was Ted. Ted was a man in his sixties. He was small in stature but big in generosity. He had thin grey hair and glasses. He was too good to be true. Ted was an employee of the tourist bureau. He didn't want to be the manager even though he had been asked to. Too much stress, he thought. He knew his job very well and was very efficient at it. And he was totally dedicated to helping his customers.

After a couple of weeks in the dreadful South Hedland Vet Clinic, I was more or less told to leave. I was supposed to do six weeks, but I had had enough. I had been treated like a bit of rubbish. I didn't know what to do next, so I phoned the tourist bureau. Ted told me, "Come in here, we'll look after you." And he really did too. I packed my bags and phoned a taxi, which picked me up and took me to the tourist bureau. Dianne never thanked me or said goodbye. I never heard from her again. I felt sorry for her; there was something very much amiss in her life, but I never could get close enough to her to find out in the short time I was there.

I arrived at the tourist bureau in the taxi feeling a bit disheartened. To walk into this homely oasis was like heaven in hell. Ted made me feel really welcome and offered me a cup of tea. I had a look around at all the brochures on the Pilbara region, the region Port Hedland was situated in. Ted showed me some of his photographs from some of the national parks he regularly visited. I could hardly believe my eyes. The spectacular gorges and waterfalls defied description! I just had to visit some of these places. Ted told me about a guy that took people on camping tours if he could get at least three people to go. I put my name on the list. I had to wait a couple of days to find out if the trip would be on. Meanwhile I decided to stay in a guesthouse that Ted had recommended in the next street over.

Sunset Lodge was easy to find. I walked over in the evening when the sun had started to lose its sting. The entrance led through a shade-cloth-covered front garden with a fish pond and a hammock to sit and enjoy the silence in. The guest house itself was very simple. It had a large central room with a skylight in the middle of the tin roof. All around the perimeter were several bedrooms, and one door led to the communal kitchen. In the central room or lounge room was the television set and the air conditioner. Here I met the landlady, Helen. She was a remarkable lady. Helen looked in her early forties, with short blond hair and a pleasing face. She spent a lot of her day sitting in a chair in front of the air conditioner. At first I thought that she seemed a bit strange. She seemed so contented and happy just to sit in her chair. Why would anyone want to spend their day in what seemed to be a daydream? And in this godforsaken place?

Helen and her husband lived in the hostel, in one of the rooms, and used the communal kitchen together with their guests. They seemed to live a very simple life. I soon found out Helen's story and why she seemed so at ease with life. A couple of years earlier she had been struck down by a life-threatening brain tumour that she had miraculously been cured from. Just simply being alive now seemed to her to be a great gift. Every day was special to her. Helen thought that Port Hedland was as nice a place as any to live in. I will always remember this person and how she taught me how differently the world can be perceived depending on our previous experiences, especially when we have been in touch with death.

After spending one night in a simple twin-share bedroom with another traveller, I walked back to the tourist bureau to see Ted. He suggested that I climb "the tower" at the back to get a bird's-eye view of Port Hedland's harbour. The tower was a sturdy steel construction with see-through stairs that spiralled up and up into the windy air. I am not partial to heights and left the uppermost storey unexplored. You had to climb up a nearly vertical ladder to reach the top. The extremely hot air tried to blow me off my feet, so I kept a firm grip of the rails all the time.

That afternoon, Ted suggested that I could stay in the caravan park, in his annex. He lived in his own little caravan permanently in the caravan park. The caravan park was situated on the beach; Ted loved swimming in the sea. This sounded OK to me. Ted's caravan was very small and worn. It had a shower inside the caravan itself. The annexe had a spare bed. It also contained all of Ted's belongings stacked up to the top. The air inside the annexe was stiflingly hot and humid and smelt of mice. To sleep at night, you had to have an electric fan directed onto your naked body. It took a bit of getting used to. The mice used to have a lot of fun at night getting into all the corn flakes. I ended up sleeping in the annexe for about a week.

Depending on the tides, Ted and I went down to the sea at different times of night or day. If the tide was out, you would have had to walk a kilometre or more to reach the water's edge. High and low tide could differ by as much as seven metres in height. But when the water came in at high tide it was only a few minutes' walk from the caravan to have a swim. We used to walk to a channel-like inlet that took the tidal water into a lot of low-lying mudflats on the other side of the caravan park. The tidal water caused a brisk flow of sea water via this channel twice daily. It was fantastic to get into the water at one end and rapidly get carried down to the other end. The beach was usually empty of people, so we didn't worry much about swimwear.

When the tide came in after dark, Ted and I used to walk barefoot down on the sand. During the day this was impossible since the sand was burning hot. We would get to the channel as the tropically warm water was rushing in. The channel got deeper and deeper and my toes would not reach the bottom. The opposite side of the channel became an ever-diminishing island. I swam across to the little island and walked around it in the pitch black without anything on. This was one of the most exotic experiences I have ever had. The water and the air were so incredibly warm! I went back into the stream. I splashed around in the water like a kid. It was unbelievably wonderful. It was supposed to be safe from sharks and other nasties in the shallows where we were. Only one little nuisance pest surprised me at first.

"Ouch! Something keeps on nipping my skin!"

"It is only the sea lice," Ted explained.

The little annoying creatures kept on pinching me. They didn't cause any bites that remained but were a bit uncomfortable as they kept on biting me, especially since I didn't have anything on protecting me!

21

A trip into the desert

The tour in a four-wheel drive vehicle that was supposed to take me to the wonderful interior of northern Western Australia never got enough people together. Instead, marvellous Ted offered to take me in his little red Suzuki! His spirit was unbelievable. He had travelled in it on many similar trips before. Fancy taking that little old car on the dirt roads into the outback. But Ted knew what he was doing. He was an extremely organised and well-prepared guy. And he knew all the national parks inside out. He had been to them many times before. How Ted managed to stack the tent, air mattresses, kitchen utensils and food and water for several days into the Suzuki defies description. But he had it all worked out and packed ready to go early the next morning.

Off we went before dawn in the little red car, with the windows wound down during the entire trip. There was no

A trip into the desert

air-con in the car. I used a wet towel onto my skin to keep cool. But the red dust came in and covered everything and everybody like red paint. We both ended up with bright red hair after a few hours on the dirt roads.

The scenery changed from flat spinifex-covered ground to stony hills. Ted pointed out a hill the locals called Tit Hill because it was shaped like a woman's breast. Tit Hill was the most prominent landmark in view for a couple of hours' driving.

This desert-like landscape was full of surprises. We now faced a sea of mud where the road was supposed to go. It didn't look as if this country ever got any rain, and here was all this mud! It was either turn back or have a go at crossing it. We choose the latter, of course. With me pushing the Suzuki from behind while Ted was showing me what the engine could do, we had her out in no time.

The next surprise was a large, beautiful waterhole called Python Pool in among the barren hills. It was the spillway of a small waterfall. It also teemed with small, nosy fish that liked to have a nibble of human legs! And they were larger, with bigger mouths, than the previous sea lice.

Our proposed camp was at the famous Millstream National Park. Here was a natural oasis that the cameleers used to visit; there were towering date palms everywhere that they had planted. Between the palms a small, crystal-clear stream was winding its way. Everything was lush and green. This must have been heaven to the hot travellers.

Some distance away was a camping area next to another amazing feature of this arid land. A huge body of spring water surfaced here, forming what looked like a wide river. It seemed to have been formed from a huge crack in the crust of the earth. The water next to the cliff edge was six metres deep. The banks were vertical, so if you jumped in you wouldn't be able to get out. Luckily there was a sturdy ladder fixed to the bank. The water was beautifully still and black and seemed bottomless. It was very clear and had little shoals of fish swimming about just below the surface. I couldn't wait to get into the water, since the temperature was a soaring 40 degrees and I was covered in the red road dust from top to toe.

Ahhh! What a life! The water was a pleasant cooling temperature and not too cold. It was not possible to reach anything to stand on; only waterweeds tickled my toes and I didn't venture far from the ladder, which was the only means of getting out of the water.

Swimming in the Millstream

Ted was already organising the erection of the tent next to the water's edge, underneath a gorgeous twisting ghost gum. This was not the tourist season, so we were the only people around. Because of the very dry and hot air it only took minutes before you dried after getting out of the water. The evaporation was so effective that it even felt too cold while the skin was wet. But it wasn't long before you longed to get back into the water again. I went up and down that ladder several times that evening.

Ted had simple eating habits. He ate straight out of a tin for dinner and ate nothing but custard (!) for breakfast. He certainly wasn't one for overindulgence. He was a rather small, wiry man. I had some tinned food as well, and then we had a last dip in the darkness and went to bed in the tent.

The heat was overwhelming, and I managed to get to sleep by putting my arm on a wet towel that acted as a cooling element. It was quite effective. I used this simple method while travelling in the car also. I wrapped a wet towel over both legs and arms. The drier the air, the better cooling effect you get. In the houses in central Australia, where the air is very hot and dry, the air conditioners worked in a similar manner, with evaporation of water only.

The next morning, we packed up and went on our way, after a last, sad dip, to the next waterhole – this time in the Karijini National Park. It was many hours' drive away. The park has many spectacular gorges, waterfalls and pools. The first visit was to Hamersley Gorge and the Spa Pool. What an apt name! It was a fairly difficult trek down to the bottom of the gorge to the river. The opposite wall of the gorge was perpendicular, and the sun was creating a masterpiece of colours and shadows upon it. Because of the depth of the gorge, part of it was in the shade.

The Spa Pool was situated upstream from where we came down to the water. Ted showed the way up and down over cliffs and overhangs. The last part took a bit of negotiating along a narrow ledge. The Spa Pool itself was one of the most magnificent natural wonders I have ever seen. It was nearly perfectly circular, with the sides curving in above to form a partial roof or cave. The rock was made up of fine layers or sediments that formed wavy shapes and patterns all around the pool. The different layers were coloured in shades of grey to red. A waterfall was pouring into the pool from above. This water had over countless aeons gouged out the rock to form the pools. The outlet was on the opposite side, forming a shallow stream in a slippery depression just excellent for sliding in or out of the pool on your belly. I could not reach the bottom anywhere, nor was there anything to stand on once in the pool. One could hang on to protruding bits of rock all along the walls instead.

In the Spa Pool

I swam across to the waterfall and put my head under the cool, crystal-clear water. There was green moss growing on the walls of the pool. It was such a paradox, so much cool

A trip into the desert

fresh water in such a hot arid place, far away from civilisation. It was hard to believe.

Ted and I climbed up to above the pool, and there were several smaller round pools of water leading in a stepwise fashion to the main one below. They were also very deep and would have been impossible to get out of without help.

After spending the rest of the afternoon splashing around in the Spa Pool, the cliff faces started to turn red in the setting sun and soon the entire gorge would turn dark with shade.

We had to leave this paradise and start the steep climb back to the car. A short drive took us to our camp for the night with a background of a red dust storm in the distance and the full moon. The campground consisted of red gravel between spinifex clumps. The spinifex grass is everywhere in this part of Australia and is extremely prickly and stiff. Some clumps were as tall as me. You have to be careful not to walk into it as it can be painful. You need sturdy foot and leg wear to be able to walk through it.

Me with a spinifex plant

The light of the full moon made it possible to go for a stroll among the tussocks of spinifex. I couldn't stop admiring the stark beauty of this harsh country. It was an eerie feeling to walk all alone so far from everything with just the night sky above in the still very hot, dry air. I can still recall that night many years later, and the feeling of insignificance one gets amid the vastness and desolation of this remote and secret part of the earth.

The next morning, we headed for yet another of this park's wonders, Dale's Gorge, with Fortescue Falls and Circular Pool. Descent down to Fortescue Falls was via a steep, narrow trail that had been built along the edge of the gorge. At the lower end the trail turned into layered rock formations that formed natural steps of different width and height. The whole place was "stepped". It reminded me of an amphitheatre. These amazing steps seemed made for walking on.

Getting into the water below Fortescue Falls was easy, as these steps continued into the large pool of turquoise water. I got into the lovely cool water via some wide, perfectly flat steps after the hot descent down the gorge trail. The air temperature was an intense 40 degrees. It was possible to walk on ever-deeper steps until they were out of reach of my feet and I had to start swimming. The gorgeous Fortescue waterfalls had to be reached by swimming a short distance. These falls are permanent and cascade down a series of natural steps as well. It was possible to climb up on the steps and sit among the rushing water. What a wonderland! I had difficulty accepting that such natural wonders actually existed. And if it hadn't been for the disastrous locum job I went for in Port Hedland, I might never have experienced this wonderland. You just don't expect an arid country to harbour such watery places.

After a couple of hours it was time to leave again and head for the next surprise. By the time I had climbed to the top of the gorge I wished I was back in the water again. It really was exhausting this time of year, but in wintertime, on the other hand, the water gets too cold to swim in. The last place to visit was Circular Pool. The view from the top of the cliffs down onto the pool was spectacular. It was azure blue and stood as a sharp contrast against the reddish rocks. It was a long way down there, and it looked like a small round coin. To get there we had to first descend another long, steep track to the bottom of Dale's Gorge and walk along the creek for a couple of hours.

Along the bottom of Dale's Gorge there were eye-catching deposits of asbestos wedged in between the layers of sedimentary rock. It formed twenty-millimetre thick, horizontal blue-green seams everywhere. There had been signs on entering the park warning about the health risks because of the asbestos deposits. In Wittenoom township there used to be mines for asbestos and lots of people developed mesothelioma, a form of cancer, as a result of being exposed to the mineral. It was a strange-looking mineral; it formed fibres that could be seen squashed on the ground everywhere in the park.

It was a long walk between thickets of lush vegetation, rock-hopping along the beautiful, flowing stream that formed lots of very wide and shallow waterfalls as it carved its way along the floor of the gorge. The approach to Circular Pool was lined with huge boulders that formed a formidable barrier to easy entry. It took some effort negotiating these boulders to even get a first glimpse of the water of the pool, let alone get into it for a swim! The boulders continued into the water, forming islands above water and ledges to stand on underwater. They were quite sharp, and Ted had a bit of an accident and cut his foot. He was bleeding profusely, and I had to be the doctor that bandaged up the foot with a shirt I had to rip apart. If you had a nasty accident here, you would be in serious trouble because of the remoteness and inaccessibility of the place.

On the opposite side of the pool there was a wide, flat rock ledge under an overhanging cliff wall. Water trickled down the wall and onto the ledge. The constant moisture and shade had given rise to a profusion of ferns and mosses. It was like being in paradise.

This was the last place I visited in the Pilbara and the memory from the four days we spent in the national parks lives vividly with me forever. The long, hot drive back to the town of Port Hedland was the close of my northern Western Australia experience.

Ted beside a termite mound

22

Monkey Mia, where dolphins meet people

The next day came the sad moment to say goodbye to Ted and board the coach, very early in the morning, to head south towards Perth. On the way down was a famous tourist destination, Monkey Mia, a resort where you can come close to wild dolphins. I had always wanted to see wild dolphins, and this was my chance.

After countless hours on the coach we finally arrived at the turnoff to Monkey Mia. Here I had to catch another bus to the very low-key resort. The resort was situated along a pristine stretch of beach and consisted of small, thatched-roof huts that blended in with the natural vegetation. Here the rangers fed the dolphins at specific times, and the tourists could partake in the event.

I had an hour's wait or so before the first dolphin appeared in the shallow water near the beach. There were twenty or so people of all ages keen to see the dolphins being fed. We were told by the ranger to walk in knee deep in the warm sea water and stand still to let the animals come up and investigate us! Dolphins are curious and playful mammals, and each one has its own personality. One old-timer in particular kept on making a show of itself and was a bit gamer than the rest. It even let people touch it gently. This pod of wild dolphins consisted of true wild animals that had gradually come to trust humans.

It was getting to late afternoon, and I was to catch a bus from the resort back down to the main road again. I had left my suitcase on the bus, as the driver reassured me it would be OK. I expected the same bus to reappear at the same spot as I previously had alighted. I got more and more worried as only a huge, different-looking coach drove up and then left from a totally different spot. There were no people to ask or buildings around as I was standing in among some shrubs. This was a deserted place. There was no designated bus stop as such or signs informing people were to wait. I started to panic, thinking I would be stranded without my luggage, and God knew where they would take it. There were no mobile phones in those days. The next bus would be in twenty-four hours. Then I noticed the bus slowing down as it turned up the hill going away, hesitate and reverse to turn around. The driver must have spotted me standing there all alone. What a relief! This was the right bus, and it had my luggage onboard as well. I was the only person on the bus. I didn't have to sleep among the sand dunes after all.

All was well again. The trip to Perth was going to take all night, with a couple of stops for refreshments on the way.

23

Cheviot Lodge

I HAD A TIP-OFF ABOUT A hostel in Perth, close to the bus station, to stay in overnight, since my connecting bus to Katanning didn't leave until the following day. I had had an offer to run a small single-vet mixed practice in Katanning in the southwest of Western Australia. It would make a full circle, since I had worked on a farm in Katanning twenty years before! At first I was a bit hesitant about the offer since I don't like retracing my steps, but I decided to check it out.

Cheviot Lodge was an old two-storey building a short walk from the bus station. I got a shared room with two other girls for eleven dollars a night. I found out that one of the girls smoked in the room, much to my disgust. The girls were long-time boarders.

The hostel had a common room downstairs with television and so on. A dubious character approached me as I was sitting in the lounge checking out some magazines. Gary was rather dirty and looked unkempt. He obviously lived long-term in the hostel. He sat himself down beside me on the couch. He opened up a huge, well-thumbed book that was barely hanging together and asked me what my birth date was. Then he brought out an impromptu bottle of wine as well! Alcohol was not permitted in the common room of the hostel, and signs on the wall pointed to this fact. He offered me a glass, which I hesitantly accepted, and filled it with wine. This guy had an amazing talent in explaining all about my stars and horoscope and about my future and personality. The big book was an astrology reference book, and Gary knew it inside out. But I suppose this was all he did all day. I was glad I only stayed the one night, since Gary got a bit too overpowering as the evening went past.

The following morning, I boarded the bus to Katanning, a five-hour journey through rolling hills with wheat and sheep farms. It was the end of a long, dry summer. The wheat had been harvested long ago. The fields were browned off and grazed down to bare ground. The country was waiting for the autumn rains that fall fairly predictably in this part of the world.

24

Arrival in Katanning

When I finally reached my destination after the five-hour bus trip, there was nobody around to pick me up. I had arranged to be picked up by the vet nurse at the bus station in Katanning. I found a phone booth and phoned the vet clinic I had come to work at. There were no mobile phones then.

"Sue is on her way," a female voice informed me. Five minutes later a yellow Volvo station wagon pulled up. The two doors on the passenger side were badly indented. One of the vets that had worked there had apparently rolled the car, so now the doors were very hard to open and shut. The car was an old bomb and had travelled twice around the clock and now the clock had given up its ghost.

Sue was a tall and heftily built girl in her early twenties. She had long, wavy brown hair that she hid behind. She tended to face the ground and raise her eyebrows as she looked up towards you. She had worked in Mitchell Vet Hospital for the last four years and had seen many vets come and go. It was hard to find vets to take up a position here in the country three hours' drive south from Perth. The clinic had sometimes been without a vet at all for periods of several weeks. I later realised that Sue had come to believe that she could do the vet's work by herself, and this is where the problems started.

About three kilometres out of town we turned into a wide gravel driveway leading up to a large corrugated iron shed. There was a tall glass sign at the turnoff that could be lit up at night with VET on it. This sign later proved to be irresistible to vandals, who would smash it by throwing bricks at it.

On the right side of the driveway was a small, dilapidated cottage named "the Palace". On the left was a horse yard with a large gum tree in the middle. To the right of the large shed was a very old, open wooden shed. In the backdrop was a grove of trees. Behind the Palace was a five-acre paddock with a huge, ugly hole dug out with a dried-out dam on the bottom. In the overgrown grass around the buildings were old tyres, sheets of galvanised iron and tin cans scattered around the place. I even found a full bottle of anaesthetic in the grass along the driveway.

In front of the large shed a faded blue sign rested sadly on the ground with MITCHELL VETERINARY HOSPITAL on it in white letters. Inside the glass front door was the reception area. It had a nice big timber reception desk, solid and well polished. There were shelves with equestrian goods for sale along the walls. The internal walls of the surgery were made of Besser blocks painted white. The reception area led into a consulting room with a large white table and a huge old fridge. Then there was an office with an old table and sink below the window, and a spacious animal room with a large set of battered, homemade galvanised two-storey cages on wheels. The concrete floor was painted a dark reddish brown. The animal room led into a narrow passageway to the old shower, which had been turned into a developing room for the x-ray films. The window had been taped up with black fabric to exclude any light.

At the end of the passage was the surgical theatre, with an old Laminex surgery table propped up on a few red bricks to gain some more height. The window looked out into the yards and a pleasant, wooded area. There were shelves everywhere, stacked neatly with drugs and equipment.

The brick walls had some substantial cracks in a few places where the foundations had settled and caused the walls to move further apart. The ceilings were precariously hanging on to the walls, which were drifting apart in several places. They were badly stained from leaking rain. The guttering to the huge shed was rusted through all around and water poured from the holes during a downpour, making the ground a quagmire and causing the foundations to move.

A door from the office led into the other half of the big shed, which contained two sand yards and two pipe crushes in which to restrain horses and cattle. There was also an old washing machine that regularly had to be stood on its head to try and pull out hair and lint from the plumbing so that it would drain. Old "Ovlov", the yellow Volvo vet car, also had its sleeping place here. The huge sliding door leading out of the shed was nearly jammed and took a huge effort to open.

Now came the big question.

"Where am I supposed to stay?" I asked Sue nervously.

"Over there," Sue answered with embarrassment in her voice. "We call it 'the Palace.'" I was afraid that this dilapidated shack would be my designated home for the next fifteen months.

***

On the eastern side of the Palace was a rendered yellow wall with cracks in it and a couple of windows covered with old fly screens that were hanging off in shreds. The guttering was absent and the weeds along the wall were thriving. Outside the front of the building was a simple bush-rail fence with a wooden gate. The walls consisted of grey asbestos sheeting that looked as if it had been tacked on by an amateur. The rusty corrugated iron roof drained into a corrugated tank on a wooden stand. The back of the Palace had another tank, without a top, which contained millions of mosquito larvae that thrived in the murky water. The western side of the Palace consisted of a taller structure, of red brick with a pitched roof, that looked totally different to the rest. It had a verandah with an overgrown flower bed in front. It looked like that was the original part of the building and the asbestos parts had been added on later bit by bit.

Upon entering the front door that led into the kitchen, I was pleasantly surprised. All the internal walls and ceilings had been freshly painted. Sue had stocked the fridge with some food. The living room was in the tall original building; it had high ceilings, three old-fashioned windows and a door leading onto the cement verandah. The internal walls had telltale marks from water that had been running down them. The floorboards were bare and were painted a yucky brown. On the floor lay a green bean bag. Next to it was a sagging old vinyl couch. There was an old telly and some old stereo equipment that kept on blowing fuses.

There were open fireplaces on opposite walls, one smaller than the other. A small rusty potbelly stove lived in the small fireplace. The walls had extensive cracks from ceiling to floor.

The kitchen had an old-fashioned stainless steel sink and an old gas stove. A sort of deep guttering ran *inside* the kitchen along the dividing wall to the rest of the building. Every time it rained this structure leaked profusely all over the benches and almost flooded the kitchen.

A step down led to a narrow hallway with three more rooms. On the right was a tiny room without floor coverings and with walls that had been patched up with paper and painted upon. The floor had remnants of some crumbling black tar-like substance.

On the left was an old-type shed door with a sliding latch leading into "the dungeon". This part of the Palace was a mess. The fibro walls were caving in with sand and soil from the outside. The louvre windows had several pieces of glass missing. There were some cardboard boxes full of bits and pieces of clothing – these came in handy, since most fitted me well. The floor was covered in a thick layer of dust and grime and millions of dead black beetles. I was to find out later that these beetles hibernated in the numerous cracks in the walls and kept on emerging onto the floors of the kitchen every day in large numbers.

At the end of the corridor was the master bedroom. It was

fairly large and had one window, with louvres that used to drive me mad on windy nights from rattling against each other. The walls were rendered and painted yellow. The low-pile, multicoloured striped carpet on the floor had not been fitted, merely laid out directly onto the concrete floor without any underfelt. The plasterboard ceiling had black water stains from mould along all the joints.

A single steel bed stood alone in the middle of the floor. An old wardrobe and two very unmatched chests of drawers, one painted bright orange, were the only bedroom furniture. I used a little green plastic stool as a bedside table.

Now, last of all, the interesting bathroom. It led on from the kitchen and had a green painted concrete floor. There was no hand basin, only a laundry tub next to an old washing machine. A set of frosted louvres let some light in. The bathtub was cast iron and stood on the floor, with the drainpipes running on top of the floor out through a hole in the wall! The enamel was sadly worn off to the rusty bottom. The plumbing to this bathroom was extraordinary in many ways. The number of pipes and brass taps everywhere would even make a plumber confused. Over the laundry tub there were one hot and three cold taps, some joined onto the same line. One pointed sideways. Low along the wall was a tap from the roof-less, mosquito-riddled rain tank. Over the bath was a hot water tap but no cold water tap. All the pipes were mounted onto the walls. If you wanted a bath you had to turn on the shower to get cold water into the bath, so the bath had to be run before you could get in, but I devised a way to wrap the shower curtain around the shower head to act as a kind of pipe into the bath. It worked reasonably well. If you weren't careful when pulling the curtain it would fall down on top of you, since the bar it was running on wasn't fixed properly.

The hole in the wall around the bath drainpipe was large enough to let various wildlife into the house. It also let in a large amount of leaf litter and dust. For towels I found some quite good ones that were brought in with sick dogs and cats, which I washed and used myself.

There were no light fittings in the house, only bare bulbs.

25

What a hillbilly show

I STARTED WORK THE SAME DAY I arrived in Katanning. It soon became clear that Sue considered herself the manager of the show. Out of necessity she had had to run the business without a vet being there for some time, so she had gradually come to consider herself to be the vet. The day I arrived I found her disappearing into the consulting room with a client. I later checked some clients' cards out and found she had been diagnosing and prescribing treatments in the past and was still expecting to do this after I arrived. I was busy on the phone, and when I finished I went in to check what was going on. I found Sue busily administering snake antivenene to a cat. I nearly felt sick. What did this young unqualified lass think she was doing? And in front of the vet and owner of the cat? What was five years of study to become a vet worth? Nothing? I worried how I would deal with this without causing tension.

I didn't want to say anything in front of the client. I let Sue finish what she was doing. When the owner had left, I carefully mentioned to Sue that I considered the veterinary work to be my responsibility. It was hard for me to come and take over the running of the place after Sue had devoted so much effort and time there. She obviously had emotional ties with Mitchell Vet Surgery and even with some of the clients and their animals. I felt like an outsider trying to work my way in and push the local staff out. Sue was born and bred in Katanning.

After a few days of getting to know each other, things started to work out the way they should, with me being the vet and Sue accepting to be the receptionist and vet assistant. Sue had learnt a lot by working with other vets and was very informative and helpful to have around. Vet nurses often have a lot of tips they can pass on to the vet. We got on very well after the initial misunderstanding was ironed out.

This clinic was not busy, but I was supposed to be there seven days a week, twenty-four hours a day. This was a big commitment on my part. Mobile phones weren't that brilliant then. I had a big cumbersome mobile supplied, but I didn't really have anywhere to go of a weekend since I didn't have my own car. I wasn't supposed to use the clinic car for private use. The mobile reception wasn't what it is today. You had to stay in town for it to work. I ended up making some local friends that could take me out sometimes. Otherwise the clinic would have felt like a prison.

The owner of the clinic also owned several other clinics around Australia. He lived in one of them down south, a few hours away. I hardly ever saw him, only on occasion when he brought up some medications and vaccines. He couldn't care less what we did as long as we made him some money. This felt good because I could pretend that it was my own place. I could do things the way I liked and not be told what to do and how to treat my patients.

26

Wyreema Jess

In the Australian countryside, where dogs lived on farms that were separated by many kilometres, farmers regarded it unnecessary to sterilise their female dogs. They seldom got unwanted puppies because it was too far for stray males to come and visit their bitches in season. Often the farmers bred their good working bitches once or twice to get a couple of litters out of them and then left the bitches entire for the rest of their lives. There was a widespread belief that desexed working bitches became fat and lazy. The following story illustrates sadly what can happen if you don't plan to breed from your bitch and don't get her desexed.

Wyreema Jess was a lovely black-and-tan Australian Kelpie bitch that had worked sheep faithfully for her master since she was a pup nine years before. She had had a litter of pups once many years earlier but had not been able to conceive since.

Jess was brought into the surgery because she had refused to eat for a couple of days. She had had a dirty-looking discharge from her vulva for some days. All she wanted to do was to lie around. She could barely walk and had to be carried into the clinic in the arms of her owner, a seasoned farmer in his forties.

"Jess has a very high fever," I said to the farmer after examining her. "Her temperature is well over 40 degrees, which is a high fever for a dog. She is very dehydrated and will need some intensive care to pull through."

I looked at Jess' owner, trying to explain carefully to him the seriousness of the situation.

"Jess has what is called pyometra, which is a life-threatening condition. The uterus or womb becomes full of deadly pus. It is like having a huge abscess internally. The toxin spreads around the body and will kill the dog."

I continued: "The only treatment is to remove the infected organ surgically. This is a very risky operation to do when Jess is already so ill." I paused to let Jess' owner take it all in.

"This is a very delicate operation, and the pus-filled organ can easily rupture and spill the pus into her abdomen. Before and after the operation Jess will have to stay in intensive care on an intravenous drip. All this can become quite expensive and there is no guarantee of her surviving the ordeal in the end."

"Do whatever you have to do," the farmer said. "She has been such a treasure. Whatever it takes, try to save her at all costs."

After stabilising Jess with lots of intravenous fluids and antibiotics I operated on her for three hours. I managed to remove a massive pus-filled uterus. It was nearly like spaying a near-term pregnant bitch. The only difference was that this uterus was full of deadly poison and not little puppies.

Jess managed to come through the surgery. She was a tough dog. Her ordeal seemed to be over. I decided to keep her in the hospital for another two days, after which she was already back to her usual bouncy self. I decided she was now fit enough to go back home.

A man other than Jess' owner had been sent in to pick Jess up.

"Now be careful and do not let Jess run around or jump for at least fourteen days until the stitches have been removed. This is *very* important," I emphasised.

After I discharged Jess, I saw the man walk over to open the door to his high truck. Jess was delighted at being let out into freedom and ran back and forth. Then the man called her over and Jess took one big leap straight up onto the passenger side. I looked on in dismay.

Half an hour later I got a phone call from Jess' owner. He said that Jess had collapsed suddenly and had died on the way home soon after being picked up from the surgery. Some people never listen.

27

Mrs Bessen is coming: Take cover!

Take cover! Here comes Mrs Bessen! When Mrs Bessen turned up at the surgery everything else that was going on had to come to a standstill. Luckily this only happened about once a month. Mrs Bessen was a dear old lady with two woolly collie dogs, who used to come to town once a week. She always seemed to have trouble getting herself organised in time, so when she had to come to the surgery she usually turned up at either lunchtime or closing time. And then she demanded the vet's attention for at least an hour. Or she'd phone you about any little query and keep you on the phone for nearly half as long.

One Saturday morning I was on my way home from a house call and it was after closing time. I met the vet nurse on the way, and she pulled me up.

"Mrs Bessen is still outside the surgery," she said with a great sense of urgency. "She's eating a banana in her car. If I were you I'd drive around the block until she has gone."

I heeded the warning and went past the surgery driveway and took a long drive around the neighbourhood. I slowly came back on a bush track behind the surgery to make sure that the coast was clear. Mrs Bessen's green Toyota was gone, so I could return with safety and spend the rest of Saturday afternoon relaxing.

On another occasion I was alone in the surgery. It was a quiet afternoon, and the vet nurse had gone home. I had only one consult booked in, a dog close to whelping. As I examined the dog another group of people turned up unannounced, clutching onto a sad-looking little black pup. Then the phone rang. I had to excuse myself in the middle of taking the pregnant bitch's rectal temperature. It was Mrs Bessen.

"Oh, is that you, Margareta. I am glad I got you on the phone." (Normally I try to avoid answering the phone if I can help it. A vet's time is usually too valuable to chat to the public about everyday things.)

"There was just something I had to ask you about …"

As she went on another couple of clients arrived to pick up their dog that had undergone surgery that day. I tried to give them a quick apologetic smile as they walked through the door. I hoped they also would understand my plight as I was having to listen to the never-ending Mrs Bessen.

"Cindy Liz has had a bath this morning." Mrs Bessen continued. "The mobile dog washer came out because I told him I'd pay the extra for him to come to Tambellup. Do you think she will get cold if I leave her in her kennel tonight? I have put lots of blankets in there. Or should I put her in the laundry? But the laundry has a concrete floor and then it may be a bit damper in there. I really don't know what would be best for her with her arthritis."

Half an hour later I managed to convince Mrs Bessen that Cindy Liz definitely would be better off in the kennel. By now the waiting clients and their animals had become a little restless and so was I. They gave me sympathetic looks, since they could follow my conversation with Mrs Bessen. I finally put the phone down with a sigh of relief. It was nearly closing time.

"How come you being the vet have to answer the phone?" one client wondered. "Don't you have a receptionist?"

28

A vet's heartache

ONE EVENING WHILE I WAS cooking tea, a Mrs Todd rang and said her poodle's front leg seemed broken. She explained to me that the leg was hanging at a funny angle and the dog could not put it down or bear weight on it. The dog's name was Brute. All he had done to sustain the injury was jump off a chair. I told Mrs Todd to bring the dog in straight away if she so wished.

Mrs Todd, a woman in her early thirties, arrived ten minutes later with a small dog in her arms. The little dog was covered in curly black hair. It was hard to see the dog's eyes among all the hair. Brute was not a brute at all. He was the most delightful fluffy creature anyone could wish for. He wagged his short, docked tail and licked my hand eagerly when I presented it to him cautiously. His left front paw was hanging limp. I gently tried to feel the leg to see if and where it might have been broken. Brute immediately started yelping at the top of his voice. He was obviously not a very brave little dog.

I explained to Mrs Todd that Brute's leg would have to be x-rayed the next day, and it would be best if the dog stayed in the hospital overnight. Mrs Todd didn't like the idea of leaving the dog behind but eventually agreed to leave him. With her holding onto Brute, I managed to put a simple bandage around the dog's injured leg to give it a bit of support overnight. Brute yelped again no matter how carefully I handled his leg. I put the patient in a small hospital cage for the night and he didn't seem to mind too much.

The next day I x-rayed Brute's leg without him even needing a sedative. He was amazingly well behaved for a little poodle. We sat him on his chest on the x-ray cassette and extended his injured leg onto the cassette with the film inside it. *Snap!* The x-ray machine made a loud noise as always, that sometimes startled the animal. Brute didn't even flinch. Then we had to lay him on his side. A lot of dogs resent being laid on their side, especially on an x-ray table. They often need to be given a general anaesthetic just to be able to take pictures of their bones. But Brute didn't mind the sideways positioning either.

What a lovable little dog, I thought. *I wish they were all this amiable.*

The x-rays showed a clean break of the radius and ulna, the two bones in the forearm. I had pinned a similar fracture in a small dog a couple of months earlier. It was a fairly tricky procedure, but the outcome was generally excellent.

I informed Mrs Todd on the best option of having the dog's leg pinned. It would not cost her more than 300 dollars. With Brute being only a young dog the chances of a full recovery were excellent. To my surprise, Mrs Todd started to tell me how Brute hadn't cost her that much and that she really didn't want to spend that much on him! I could hardly believe my ears. With hesitation she agreed to have Brute's leg pinned. She took him home for the night and was supposed to bring him back in the morning for the operation.

I made up a huge pack of bone pins, drapes and instrument to be sterilised for several hours in preparation for the next day.

The next morning Mrs Todd rang and said she and her husband had decided they didn't want to spend any more money on Brute. They had given the delightful little dog to some farmers to do away with. It was a bizarre ending to a heartbreaking story. I was never sure whether to believe in Mrs Todd's last words or not. If she wanted the dog put down and if she cared at all, wouldn't it have been more dignified to have the vet put it to sleep?

29

The Sawyers

It was Saturday afternoon. The surgery was basically closed, but since I lived next to the clinic at the time, just outside Katanning, people would sometimes just turn up without phoning first. That was always a problem with living at the premises.

I was just making myself a cup of tea when a car pulled up in front of my cottage. It was Mr and Mrs Sawyer, an elderly couple. I had treated their little Maltese-cross dog, Cindy, some weeks earlier for a skin complaint. Cindy was their beloved companion and they both shared a passion for her. So great was their love for Cindy that they seemed to share the same thoughts about the little dog. When Mrs Sawyer started a sentence Mr Sawyer would take it up halfway and vice versa.

"Cindy just won't stop scratching," Mrs Sawyer said in a

broad British accent ...

"And it is driving her mad," Mr Sawyer added.

"Did the tablets work that I gave her before?" I asked.

"Oh yes," Mrs Sawyer said ...

"But as soon as they were finished, she started again," Mr Sawyer went on.

"She has got a red spot on her back, and I have been putting that cream on it," Mrs Sawyer said ...

"But it does no good," Mr Sawyer continued.

"She can't go on like this," Mrs Sawyer complained. "Maybe a needle would work."

"Why not give it a go?" Mr Sawyer finished.

Meanwhile, Cindy was bouncing around our feet panting and yelping excitedly. She was a delightful little dog with a friendly temperament, contrary to many dogs of her type.

After Cindy was dealt with, Mr Sawyer went on to talk about the couple's previous dog, a border collie cross that had passed on some time ago. I listened patiently, thinking about my by now cold cup of tea.

"Buster was six-year-old," Mr Sawyer continued, "and he went just like that." He snapped his fingers. "It was strange how he was as good as gold one day and dead the next."

Mrs Sawyer had resigned from the conversation and seated herself in a chair in the surgery. Buster had obviously been a favourite of her husband.

"What happened to him, then?" I asked Mr Sawyer.

"Cancer," he answered. "I didn't think a dog could go that quickly. It's frightening. He started vomiting blood one morning and we took him to the vet, but he died that afternoon. It makes you worry about Cindy."

"Don't worry about Cindy," I said. "I had a Maltese cross dog here recently that was eighteen years old. Terriers can be tough little nuts." The couple finally left. I had to re-heat my cup of tea again.

30

A learning curve like no other

When I started at Mitchell Vet Hospital in Katanning, I did not know anything about ostriches. I had never treated one before. The same goes for ostriches as for everything else; you learn on the job. I did not bring any literature to Katanning from Queensland. As a matter of fact I did not bring much of anything, since I flew over. Luckily the previous vet, who was a female about my size, left a lot of clothing that I fitted into very well. Thank you very much, Dr T!

Getting back to the ostriches, I was called out to see one on a farm about forty-five minutes' drive from the surgery. It was an eighteen-month-old female "with something hanging out and dripping from her bottom," the farmer informed me.

I got on the phone to a vet that was supposed to know a lot about ostriches. I was informed that female ostriches often get a prolapse of the oviduct and it *looks like a pink tennis ball full of fluid,* and all you have to do is *stab the ball with a scalpel blade to drain the fluid out* and presto, the problem is fixed!

Armed with this important information, I set out to see the ostrich. I arrived an hour later at what looked like Old MacDonald's Farm. Apart from the ostriches there were deer, ponies, cows, emus, kangaroos, sheep, ducks, turkeys and more. Amalda, the ostrich hen, was in a very large pen with a huge male bird. I could envisage myself on the ground with this impressive two-legged feathered creature standing on top of me with its huge clawed feet pinning me down.

"Now how are we going to catch the hen?" I asked the farmer.

"Oh, we'll corner her on the fence and hold her down; she doesn't usually kick up too much fuss. As long as you don't grab her from directly in front, she can't kick you. They can disembowel you with their sharp claws in one strike if you get in front of them."

I got a bigger and bigger dislike for Amalda the ostrich the more I looked at her hefty naked thighs with those scaly long legs underneath. I could see some ragged bits of something hanging from her bare behind.

Luckily I didn't have to help round up Amalda, since Farmer MacDonald found an offsider to help with the task. Amalda was more cooperative than I expected, and she was soon restrained, sitting on the ground. I examined the ragged bits of tissue from her vent. It bore no resemblance to a tennis ball whatsoever and had no fluid in it. It went back into its proper place with very little persuasion by my hands pushing it back in. I advised the farmer to observe the bird closely and to slip the lump back in if it came back out. Amalda got up and walked away as if nothing had happened. Her mate had been sulking in the far reaches of the pen during the whole procedure and seemed far more distressed than Amalda.

Unfortunately the conservative treatment didn't work on Amalda. The prolapsed cloaca (similar to a rectum in mammals) wouldn't stay in, even after being put back in several times by the owner. So Amalda was coming into the surgery in a horse float for a second treatment.

I decided to keep the prolapsed bit of tissue in via a purse string suture, contrary to advice from articles on similar matters. Amalda was again very cooperative and stood in the horse float with her rear facing the ramp with her owner restraining her. With the help of some local anaesthetic, I put in two lots of sutures under the skin encompassing the cloacal opening. Amalda didn't seem to mind one little bit. After replacing the swollen and traumatised tissue I tightened the sutures so the cloacal opening was too narrow for it to come back out. Everything went very well with this particular procedure. But now the fun started.

Amalda had incurred a long, nasty-looking slit in the skin of her neck a couple of days earlier. Could I please sew it together while the bird was here? "Sure," I said. We had to unload Amalda onto the concrete floor of the large animal part of the surgery so I could get to her neck.

An ostrich's neck is the most vulnerable part of its anatomy. It is long and narrow with a thin skin, and the bird hates having someone handling it. The long, powerful legs, on the other hand, with their sharp toenails, can inflict a lot of damage. A struggling ostrich on a slippery concrete floor tends to lose synchronisation of legs and neck. The ostrich hen had now gone down on her belly on the floor with her owner trying to hold her still. Her neck was oscillating on the floor like a captured snake and her huge feet were clambering for footing. She managed to open up a long slit in the skin of the neck with one of her claws. So now she had two slits in the neck, one on each side! Needless to say, we gave away the idea of suturing the neck, hoping the two slits would heal by themselves.

Two months later Amalda was doing fine. The neck had healed by itself and the prolapse never recurred after the farmer removed the sutures, as instructed, two days after they were put in.

31

Mr Moore's ostriches: You can't win them all

At the time I was working in the Katanning clinic, keeping ostriches and trying to breed them was popular because of their then high prices.

Mr Moore was an ostrich breeder who seemed to have an unfair number of problems with his ostriches. He had one breeder pair that produced plenty of fertile eggs. The eggs were fumigated with formaldehyde as they were put in the incubator. The chicks hatched on time and were nice and strong. But after three to four weeks, they started to lie down and pant with their necks bent backwards. I was presented with the first one just before Christmas 1996.

"He was fine this morning but by lunchtime he was lying like this and panting as if it was a really hot day, but it's not hot at all today! I can't understand it," Mr Moore said in a very fast and incoherent speech.

He was somewhat deaf and a bit hard to get through to. I examined the fluffy, ungainly creature with its beautiful big brown eyes. It was incapable of standing and had little control of its long, contorted neck.

"He is panting because he is very ill, it is not to do with the weather," I tried to explain. "I think he is on his way out. I'll see what I can do for him, but I don't hold very great hopes."

I admitted the little creature to start him on a rehydration course. I scratched around in the surgery cupboards, which had a wealth of odd bits and pieces, to find a plastic tube that would be suitable to put down the neck of the bird. I then managed to give the ostrich chick some water with electrolytes directly into his stomach via the tube. He was put on a heat pad and given antibiotics as well. He slowly deteriorated during the day and was dead the next morning, so I performed an autopsy hoping to find the cause of death. Everything looked normal so I sent some samples to the pathology laboratory. They found changes pointing towards enteritis, and also some funny changes in the brain similar to "mad cow disease" (bovine spongiform encephalopathy)! Fancy that. Mad ostrich disease. Maybe we were on to something new. Samples of brain were sent to South Australia for electron microscopy to look for the elusive causative organism of mad cow disease, which is not even a virus or bacterium.

A couple of weeks later Mr Moore turned up with another ostrich chick with identical symptoms. It had a contorted neck and had difficulty standing. I treated it in the same manner as the previous one but to no avail. It didn't last the night either. It was also autopsied and sent to the lab for further tests. I now advised that the next sick bird should be killed and samples taken from the freshly killed carcass. This way we might be able to isolate the germ that caused the deadly enteritis. I even sent Mr Moore directly down to Albany to the laboratory with the next two sick birds on the long list of casualties.

It seemed that every ostrich chick that Mr Moore had went the same way. His breeder was laying well and he had plenty of eggs to set in the incubator, but he couldn't get any chicks past the age of two months. We were all pulling our hair out in despair at not being able to come up with anything to stop the waste of chicks. We tried water medication, probiotics and electrolytes, and advised on hygiene.

For a few weeks we didn't hear from Mr Moore. We all hoped and prayed that the problem had gone away. It was too tough to tackle. Then one day I got a phone call from the vet in the next town.

"I have one of Mr Moore's ostrich chicks here. I believe you have had a few of his before."

"I sure have, and I have not had any success. They all die overnight. I have given them electrolytes and antibiotics and kept them warm, but they just don't seem to want to make it. Thanks for letting me know. I suppose Mr Moore is desperate for an answer. Unfortunately there is no simple answer or miracle cure. It is just one of these things. Everyone wants a simple cure."

Later the same day Mr Moore turned up at the surgery wanting to get some more hospital disinfectant. He never mentioned about taking an ostrich to my colleague. He kept raving on in his usually incoherent manner. It was hard to explain to him that there was not always an easy solution. I gave him a long list of things to go through systematically at home and write everything down that he was doing and when and how, and so on. Then over time we might be able to work out what he could be doing wrong. I also told him to get some chicks from another breeding pair to see if they maybe would be stronger. Maybe his breeders had some weak genetic makeup. He thanked me for that bit of advice and went on his way.

The next day my colleague phoned to say the ostrich chick she had treated by giving it electrolytes had recovered, and it had been sent home!

You can't win them all.

32

Horse trials: What could go wrong?

I HAD BEEN ASKED TO ATTEND at the one day event at a place outside Katanning called Carrolup. This is where the regular Pony Club meetings were usually held. The setting was beautiful, with lots of old trees and an old sandstone church that was converted into a hall. The grass was green this time of year, so there wasn't the usual dust typical of this part of the world for about a third of the year.

The one day event was held on a Sunday and was usually an easy job where you just had to be there and watch the action or generally take it easy. Nothing ever went wrong. This day was to be different.

The day started at 9 am with a cross-country course. There were several grades, with the more advanced competitors starting first. The grounds were full of beautifully turned out horses, from big thoroughbreds to little Shetland ponies. There were competitors of all ages and from all over Western Australia.

I settled in at the finishing point together with the judges and the like. The first starter had gone around the course and was heading for home at a flat gallop downhill. I admired the courage of these often very young riders on great big thundering horses. They flew over the jumps without a care in the world. I had done a lot of riding myself over the years but could never quite get up the nerve for jumps of any height. Another two horses were still out on the course when the fourth started.

About fifteen minutes later, when the seventh horse had just left, I got a call on the two-way radio to attend a horse at jump number six. Apparently the horse was down. My heart jumped with apprehension of what could have possibly happened. Jump number six was way up along the course. I didn't know where it was or how to get there. As I am writing this I feel the same horrible feeling of doom as I did at that time. I drove the battered business vehicle on the bumpy ground under and between the numerous trees and parked vehicles on the grounds, trying to avoid fallen branches in the long grass as I hurried along. My mind was racing, expecting the worse to have happened.

On arrival at the fateful scene, dread of all dreads! There was a large crowd of people assembled around a horse lying flat on its side. As I got out of the car and hurried over to the horse, I recognised the young woman crouching down by the horse's head stroking it helplessly. Tears were falling from her eyes onto the horse. My own heart rate must have been double the normal as I checked the pulse and heart rate of the recumbent horse. I could hear my own heart pounding through the stethoscope. Once I got hands-on with the case I sprang into action mode. I decided to inject a potent painkiller in the horse's jugular vein. Then I examined the patient's pupils, neck, spine, tail and the four legs but couldn't find anything abnormal. I asked the bystanders exactly what had happened. One person said the horse had just touched down past the jump and then it seemed to have stumbled for a couple of strides before it went down. Another person said it had somersaulted before it came down. I asked the girl who was crouching next to the horse (she was the rider and owner of the animal) if the horse had come down on its neck, but she was too shocked to remember anything of what had happened.

I now asked the people to help the horse on his feet to see if he could get up at all. They sat him up and gave him a push and a tug. At this stage I should have recognised the problem, because the horse failed to extend the foreleg that had been under-most. I was that distressed at the time that this important clue went into my subconscious, only to surface later. As every horse owner knows, horses get off the ground by first extending both forelegs and then pushing themselves up with their hind legs. (Cattle do the opposite; they raise the hind end first and then unfold one foreleg at a time.) So the horse failed to get up.

The veterinarian that usually treated this horse was also competing at Carrolup that day. He came over to assist as well. He ordered the horse be turned over. In the process the animal went into a violent struggling fit, thrashing madly with all four legs, spinning around on the ground while thrashing. After a few minutes it settled down enough to be approached again. It was now very apparent that the shoulder it had been lying on was broken, because the whole foreleg could be lifted up sideways. The vet looked at the owner, who was his longstanding client.

"I am sorry, Kathy," he said.

Kathy was by now hysterical, with tears flooding down her face. Her horse had been her constant companion for over ten years. They had competed at countless shows together. This was a sad ending to a long relationship indeed.

I had been rushing over to get the "green dream", or euthanasia solution. I got out of putting the horse out of his misery by handing the task to the other vet. I felt a bit guilty about it afterwards, because no vet likes to put an animal down. And it is even worse when you have gotten to know the patient. It was the one part of our professional responsibility as vets that really affected me badly.

The other vet explained to the bystanders that there could be some movements and gasping as the horse went into a deep sleep, never to wake up again.

Everything went peacefully without the dreaded thrashing that sometimes accompanies euthanasia and makes it look like a violent death. The dead body was dragged onto a float and carted away. The competition continued without a hitch for the rest of the day. To me it had been a day to remember. This had been my first public attendance as a vet, and I hoped that this would be the last time I had to be involved in a similar situation.

33

Losing one of my own horses

IN THE CONTEXT OF THE previous story at the horse trials, I remember the sad loss of one of my own beloved equine friends. Before I became a vet, I had a lot to do with horses and cattle. For many years I was running a cattle stud and used horses every day to work the cattle. I got fond of the Australian quarter horse and wanted to breed a few of my own. I bought a palomino first-cross filly from a stud in Scone in New South Wales in 1975. I had previously taught myself how to ride and break horses in, so I handled and trained this beautiful filly myself. Amber proved to be a gem. She was from a cutting-horse strain and had inherited this trait herself. Cutting horses know instinctively how to work and outsmart cattle. This makes the cattle work so much easier than on an ordinary horse. I used to live for my cattle work; now I had a smart mare to do it on.

A couple of years down the track I decided to breed Amber to a purebred quarter horse stallion. Her first foal was a chestnut filly I called Nellie. She was registered as a second-cross quarter horse. Nellie turned out to be even smarter than her mum. As a six-year-old, Nellie in turn produced a purebred chestnut filly foal.

One morning when Nellie's foal was three months old, all the other horses were coming home as usual at about ten in the morning for their morning drink. Nellie and her foal were nowhere to be seen. I always worried when the horses' usual routine was different. About half an hour later Nellie turned up, slowly dragging one hind leg. She had an anxious expression on her face. I rushed over to her to find out what was going on. Then I saw that her left thigh was very swollen, and blood was oozing from underneath. She was too sore to move. I bent down between her back legs and could see this huge hole into the muscles, just missing the belly. She nevertheless let the foal suckle from her somewhat swollen udder. The first thing into my mind was, where could she have found a stake to inflict such a horrific injury? A week earlier I had gone right around the hilly, tree-covered horse paddock with a saw and cut off any sharp bits of wood, usually an upturned tree stump that could possibly injure a horse.

After giving emergency treatment to the mare, I went out into the horse paddock to see if I could find a clue as to what had caused the nasty injury. I walked all over it, searching. There was a well-used track into a gully where the horses used to gallop down the hill. In the long grass I spotted a freshly broken-off, upright root on the ground, almost a metre long with two very sharp prongs at the tip. It had been snapped off from an upturned tree stump that still had the very weathered roots sticking out of it. The horse must have galloped right over it in the dark and caught the sharp prong with its fleshy thigh. I took it home with me. I couldn't believe that after me going around and removing every dangerous object I could find, Nellie managed to find the only one I had missed!

There wasn't much I could do for Nellie other than giving her painkillers and antibiotics. The stick had gone in really deep, but there couldn't have been a piece left in her flesh because the tip was intact on the root. The bleeding had stopped, but the thigh and hindquarter on that side kept getting larger and larger. Nellie wasn't interested in food and kept lying down looking at her injured leg. Her foal kept annoying her, not understanding why her mum was acting so strangely. I spent all day comforting both of them and offering food and water. After darkness fell I could hear Nellie through the thin weather board walls of my cottage, pawing aimlessly at the ground.

I hardly had any sleep all night. I was constantly getting up checking on Nellie and her foal. In the morning Nellie's left hindquarter had swelled grotesquely. But nevertheless, she slowly wandered off, nibbling at grass. Later in the day I felt her skin. It was cold and clammy with sweat. It was not a good sign! It could be an indication of shock setting in. Shock in medical terms means a failure of the cardiovascular system to pump blood around the body, either because of loss of excess blood or fluid, or a failure to keep the blood pressure up from a range of other factors.

It was starting to go dark. The foal wanted to play one minute and then have a drink of milk the next. Nellie's milk supply had dropped to almost nil, and the foal was getting annoyed about it, constantly trying to nibble at the udder. But mum had lost interest in her foal. She couldn't even be bothered to discipline it like mares do when they have had enough of their foal's overzealous attempts to suckle.

I walked out into the dark to check on Nellie and couldn't find her at first in the small house paddock she was in. The air had an eerie chill to it. I shone the torch around and caught sight of a dark object on the ground. Nellie had gone down next to the driveway up to the cottage. I ran over to her, stumbling in the dark. I could hear her laboured breathing as I approached her. The foal was pacing about in the dark, seemingly bewildered. Nellie's head was resting flat on the ground and there was white foam around her nostrils.

I was struck with indescribable grief as I saw my beautiful darling mare lying helplessly on the ground. I sat down by her head and stroked it gently. Her eyes were glazed, and her lungs were pumping air in and out frantically, producing the white foam around her muzzle. After a few minutes she let out a groan and started moving her legs as if trying to get to her feet. All of a sudden her whole body made a final attempt to fight off death by trying to get up and run away as horses do when they are frightened. She managed to give one almighty thrust with her hind legs, but her front legs wouldn't cooperate. With her head still bent under, her body catapulted into the air and then made a complete somersault. With a loud thud her body hit the ground for the last time. The roar of her last few breaths was deafening. Then suddenly, the stillness of the night became apparent. Her struggle was over. I sat down on the dew-covered ground and put her lifeless head in my lap.

"Not Nellie, not you Nellie!" I screamed and cried hysterically. I was paralysed with grief. I don't know how long I was sitting there stroking Nellie's head. She was my baby. She was the first foal I had ever bred. She was only six years old. But at least I had a filly foal from her. She was a spitting image of her mum. And at least the foal was three months old. She was old enough to be weaned.

The foal was whinnying for her mum. Where had mum gone? The young foal could not connect the lifeless body on the ground with her mother's warm and spirited personality.

The foal forgot her mother in two days and thrived on a diet of lucerne hay and oats. I never could forget Nellie. As I read this, I cannot help but cry again when remembering the feeling of the immense loss of the most beautiful horse there ever was.

34

How persistence wins

In sandy areas of Australia, horses tend to pick up a lot of sand off the ground and it can often upset their intricate digestive system. This is especially true when the fresh green grass comes through at the break of the season and the short pick means the horses have to graze closer to the ground to get to the succulent feed. Some horses can sometimes be seen passing pure sand. The sand can cause irritation to the bowel, with diarrhoea or worse. It can also cause a blockage and subsequent colic or gut pain.

Many horse owners opt to have their horses drenched for prophylactic purposes at the risky times of year. The drench we mostly used in Western Australia was liquid paraffin oil. We got it in forty-four-gallon drums with a hand pump on top. The oil is not absorbed by the gut lining, so it acts as a lubricant and helps pass the sand out of the horse's digestive tract. Fairly large quantities are needed, so this has to be administered via a tube inserted into one nostril and down the neck into the stomach. The nose is easier to use than the mouth because it has no teeth! Most horses will allow you to pass a tube into their nose, mostly with the help of a twitch around their upper lip to take their mind off the actual tubing procedure. A twitch is a loop of rope at the end of a long handle. The loop is passed around the horse's top lip and tightened. Some horses, though, won't let you put a twitch on their nose in the first place, and they are a real problem.

One day a woman arrived with three horses she wanted "oiled".

"We'd better start with this one." Mrs Harris pointed at the grey-white Arab mare she was hanging on to. "She's the bad one."

"We have a horse bay to do her in," I said hopefully.

"No, she won't go in one of those. She'll kill herself if you try to put her in one. She'll rear and try to climb out. We've tried it before."

"Well, we can do her here outside the clinic then, where there is plenty of space," I said.

I hated handling uncooperative or flighty horses in restricted spaces where you can't get out of their way easily.

The fine-boned little Arab mare was scanning the surrounds with wide-open eyes and flaring nostrils. Her head was held as high as it would go on the finely arched neck. Her feet were incessantly taking little steps in a small circle around her handler.

I was trying the pretty mare out to see if she was head shy or not. She let me rub her head and muzzle without any protest.

"Will she take a twitch?" I asked with anticipation.

"She doesn't like a twitch. She keeps on throwing her head high in the air until it comes off."

After trying to put a twitch around the mare's upper lip for over half an hour I concluded that Mrs Harris was right. Every time the twitch was put in place the mare jerked her head sky high in the air while running backwards, until it was impossible to keep the twitch in place.

"I think you are right. She certainly doesn't like the twitch. And she is a cunning little sod the way she knows how to beat us. I don't like sedating horses for tubing, but I may have to," I said to Mrs Harris.

"I rather you didn't," Mrs Harris replied. She has been tubed before without anything like that. I want to teach this mare a lesson. I don't like her beating us all the time."

I fully agreed with that. If you let a horse beat you at any time it will remember and get more and more determined to have its own way each time it has a win.

Mrs Harris then asked if she could have the long drenching tube. She held the mare in one hand and the tip of the tube in the other. Every time she tried to put the tube against the mare's nostrils the mare threw her head up in the air and danced around in a circle around her handler. The mare was determined not to have anything to do with the tube. Every time she tried to get away Mrs Harris followed by persistently keeping the tube up against the mare's nostril. At certain moments the mare got a touch up with the whip, which made her run around frantically at the end of the lead. She had been spoilt by getting her own way before and was now getting a much-needed lesson who was the boss.

After at least an hour of this performance the Arab mare started to give in. She realised that she wasn't going to get anywhere by resisting. The perseverance and consistency of her handler was paying off. Both the handler and the horse were by now exhausted. I carefully walked up to the mare. I could now at last insert the tube into the mare's nose without any trouble. It only took a couple of minutes to complete the drenching with several litres of paraffin oil.

After the Arab mare was done, I drenched the other two, *easy* horses in a few minutes. The whole exercise had taken most of the afternoon. But at least we had won over the mare's stubbornness. This incident goes to show you how patience, perseverance and consistency are all traits that go a long way when dealing with our equine friends.

35

The fragility of horses

ONE OF THE MOST DREADED things a vet can be asked to deal with is a horse with serious colic. Colic simply means belly ache. Horses are very prone to suffer from belly aches, for two reasons. Firstly, they have a low pain threshold, and secondly their intricate and very large digestive system is prone to problems by way of its design. Colic can be caused by a simple bowel impaction to a severe strangulation of the small bowel. Internal parasites can also cause severe bellyache with diarrhoea and even a perforation of the bowel, which means certain death.

One Sunday morning at six o'clock I got a distressed phone call:

"My trotting filly has had colic since last night and I have been up with her all night, walking her around so she doesn't go down and roll. We drenched her with oil last night. She doesn't seem to be getting any better. Can we bring her over?"

The horse only lived about two kilometres from the vet surgery.

"Sure, bring her over straight away."

I got out of bed and got dressed in a hurry and walked over to the surgery to get things ready to receive the big patient. The clinic had a horse stall under the main roof with a sand floor to keep horses in for observation if needed. I hadn't used the stall more than a couple of times in the past twelve months. Five minutes later the people rang again:

"I don't think the filly will make the journey, she is in that much pain. Can you come over here?"

I packed all the gear I might need in the old Volvo in a hurry and drove over. The woman's husband was leading the little bay filly around in a small paddock. The filly was only a two-year-old and hadn't been to the track as yet but had been getting regular workouts. As the filly was being led, she almost stumbled along. She looked as if drunk. I walked up to her to give her a brief examination, but it proved impossible as every time I tried to put my hand on her she responded by trying to throw herself on me. It was more than likely intense internal pain causing her to behave in this strange way.

I decided to give her a potent pain killer into the jugular vein if possible. Luckily the spasmodic pain must have abated for a short while, so I managed to give the injection without being trampled. I also managed to examine her reasonably well. Most vital parameters seemed surprisingly normal apart from her not having passed any of the oil she had been drenched with the night before. Also, when I did a rectal palpation of her insides, I found an empty bowel except for in the left hip area where I could feel an impacted mass. I started to suspect a severely impacted bowel or an infarction, not uncommon in equines of all ages. An infarction could be caused by worms blocking off the main artery to the large intestine, causing it to stop working. This filly would need surgery as a treatment and it was not an option in this case, so all we could do was to wait and see if the oil was going to work or not.

After the pain killer took effect, the filly seemed to be free of pain at last and was standing quietly resting after her long ordeal. I got ready to leave and told the owners to contact me if the horse got painful again.

Four hours later the filly's owner called me. She said the filly had started to roll violently again. She must have passed some oil since her buttocks were stained with it.

I returned to the property again and gave the horse another dose of pain killer. This time it didn't have any effect at all. The filly was obviously in agony since it was nearly impossible to keep her on her feet. All she wanted to do was to go down and roll. I had to give her another, stronger drug to see if that would help. The only way I could get it into her was while she had gone down and with the man holding her head down. This injection at last helped the filly settle enough so I could examine her again.

I decided to give the filly some more oil and fluids via a nose tube while she was lying down, since the last lot of oil eventually had come through. Nothing but oil had been evacuated from her bowels for ten hours, which was alarming. Maybe she had a very bad impaction that the oil managed to pass through? Hopefully the impaction would eventually shift. We could only hope, but it didn't look good at this stage. I went back home again to get some very late breakfast at 1 pm.

At 4 pm the horse was still no better. If anything she seemed worse. She still hadn't passed any manure and was impossible to keep on her feet. When I arrived, the filly was lying dead still upside down and with all four feet in the air. Her head was stretched right out with the underside of her throat uppermost. It looked bizarre. The man was standing at the end of the lead rope watching helplessly. The situation was clear. The filly would have to be euthanised.

It was a struggle to get the filly back on her feet again. She was a lather of sweat when we managed to get her up. She was to be put down further down the paddock where she could be buried. She was that violent at this stage that she was a real danger to her handlers and the vet. She wouldn't let anyone touch her without instantly trying to throw herself towards the person again. I managed to quickly deliver a jab in the side of the neck with a sedative that hopefully would make her approachable for a long enough time to give the two large syringes with euthanasia solution, which is a type of concentrated anaesthetic, into her jugular vein and put her to sleep for ever.

About half an hour later the filly was ready to receive the injection that would free her from all pain for good. The woman who owned the filly didn't want to be present when her beloved horse was being put to sleep. She had actually bred the filly and raised her from a foal. She was nearly hysterical with grief. This was the second offspring from the same mare that had to be put down. A couple of weeks earlier the filly's sister had got tangled in a fence and ripped her leg so badly that she had to be destroyed. And now this one had to be destroyed as well. It didn't seem fair. I felt a lot of sympathy for the owners of this promising young filly.

The filly stood totally exhausted while I rapidly gave her the lethal injection into her jugular. In about thirty seconds she dropped onto the ground where she was to be buried and gave a final gasp. Then everything was still. She was free at last. Darkness had set in, and the air had changed from warm to chilly.

Now came the gruesome task of performing a post-mortem. The owners wanted to know exactly what had happened inside their filly in case there was something they had done wrong that could have been prevented. Half an hour later I found the reason for the intense pain the filly had been in. Half a metre of bowel had infarcted, or died, and was on the point of rupturing. There was nothing that could have been done to save this filly. A bowel infarction is usually caused by a worm that travels around in the horse's arteries and forms a blockage in the blood supply to a section of bowel, which consequently stops functioning and then quickly becomes gangrenous.

The paradox of this story is that here was an owner that cared more than anything for her horses. They had the best of care any horse would wish for and they all got wormed every six weeks which is more than most horses ever got. And her horse dies from bowel disease caused by worms! Life can certainly be cruel and unfair sometimes.

36

Bulldogs in love

CHARLIE AND CHINNY WERE A pair of white, friendly, snoring bulldogs in love with each other. Their owner dearly wanted Chinny, the bitch, to have little bulldog puppies, but Charlie didn't seem to know how to go about getting Chinny pregnant. Whenever Chinny came into season Charlie would be huffing and puffing and snoring and roaring, getting more and more excited as Chinny approached ovulation. Chinny used to prance before poor Charlie and turn her rear enticingly towards him. However, Charlie would get so excited trying to mount Chinny that he would faint from running out of air and fall flat over on his side for a short time.

Charlie and Chinny's owner rang me one day without forewarning and asked if I could artificially inseminate (AI) his bulldogs straight away. He explained the difficulty with Charlie the male bulldog.

"He is just too stupid for words. He works himself up that much. Sometimes when he does manage to mount Chinny, her back legs fold under the weight and they both end up on the floor. Then it takes him an hour to recover enough energy to have another go."

"Has Chinny ever had pups before?"

"The dog next door got to her last season, and she had to have a caesarean section to remove the puppies."

"Bulldogs are prone to difficulties with whelping. At least we know she is capable of conceiving and carrying pups to term."

I told Mr Cheetham, the owner, that I didn't have any specific equipment for AI in dogs but I would have a go. He would have to leave the two dogs in for at least a week. Luckily we had some good dog kennels at the clinic that they could be housed in. And the neighbours wouldn't complain because of barking, since bulldogs are practically incapable of making much noise. The worst noise they make is a constant snoring caused by them trying to breathe via a deformed oro-nasal anatomy. This fact would explain why Charlie would faint under stress. He couldn't get enough oxygen to meet the increase in demand during physical activity such as mounting a female. The inside of a bulldog's throat has as much loose tissue as a dog with a long nose, but the tissue doesn't quite fit into the squashed nose of a bulldog, so it tends to get in the way of the air flow to the lungs.

When the dog couple arrived, I had to quietly think to myself: *It takes a mother to love anything like that!* Charlie's extremely wide-set, bowed-out forelegs reminded me of the stance of a large reptile. His squashed-in nose had lots of deep skin folds from all the excess skin trying to fit onto a nearly non-existent snout. The skin folds had lost their hair and were discoloured from the constant rubbing together. Charlie's lower jaw was overlapping the upper jaw, and the bite of his teeth was totally out of line, giving the dog a grotesque appearance.

Contrary to their looks, these two bulldogs had the most friendly and lovable nature one could wish for. They were wagging their docked tail stumps frenetically and roaring with excitement on arrival at the vet surgery.

I decided to keep the pair apart in the kennels so that Charlie's libido would be as high as possible at the time of collecting his semen.

The next morning everything went according to plan. I collected an ejaculate directly into a warm, sterile jar by rubbing the foreskin of Charlie's penis. By placing a small drop of semen on a microscope slide and looking at it under low power, I confirmed that Charlie's semen had good motility. This fact showed up as a circular swirling movement. I then took a cut-off plastic catheter used to inseminate cattle. With a syringe attached to one end I drew up the semen from the sterile jar into the catheter and emptied it deep into Chinny's vagina. This procedure was repeated every couple of days until Chinny went off heat.

Then the waiting game came to see the results of our efforts. The gestation period for a dog is sixty-three days from ovulation, or when the bitch's egg is released from the ovary. I promised the owner that I would be around for the big event. I was going to perform a caesarean at the first sign of Chinny going into labour. I just hoped that it wouldn't happen in the middle of the night!

Time went past and I didn't hear anything from the owner

of the two bulldogs for over two months. It was well over the sixty-three days, and I had spent the last week twenty-four hours a day within easy reach of the telephone. I had tried to phone Mr Cheetham for days but hadn't been able to get through. When I eventually managed to contact him, he told me that Chinny had gone into labour on day fifty-eight from the first insemination and produced two dead pups soon after. Then she produced one live pup the same evening. The next morning the pup was nowhere to be found. The only feasible explanation to the disappearance of the last pup was that the bitch must have eaten it!

So much for that. Mr Cheetham was understandably very disappointed. I don't know whether he ever wanted to try breeding from Chinny again after that episode.

37

A happy story of a little bird

THE OTHER DAY A WOMAN brought in a pet weiro, the local name for a cockatiel. (Wild cockatiels occur in inland Australia and are now domesticated and kept as pets all over the world.) The weiro had flown into a window. It was her beloved pet bird, and it was in a sad state indeed. The bird was unable to sit up and was trembling violently. Its neck and head were twisted in a contorted way to the right, so the head was almost upside down. If let go, it would flutter uncontrollably all over the floor. I told the owner that I would do anything I could for it but didn't give her very high hopes about the bird's recovery. If it recovered at all, it might end up with some permanent disabilities.

The young bird went into violent convulsions as I tried to make it comfortable on a towel in the bottom of a cat cage.

I hurried to get some diazepam, an injectable sedative, and administered it into the pectoral, or chest, muscles as well as some cortisone.

A few minutes later the bird was relaxing totally with eyes closed, almost as if in a deep sleep. I dropped some water into its beak, which it eagerly drank. I left it alone in the dark in the x-ray developing room, which also served as the isolation ward.

Several hours later the sedative started to wear off and the bird started to tremble again. It had an anxious expression on its face, not understanding what was happening to it, wondering why its legs wouldn't work anymore. I managed to feed the poor patient some mushy parrot food. Then I gave him, because I think he was going to develop into a male, another injection of sedative.

Lyn, the vet nurse, was looking on in disbelief. "Is he ever going to recover?"

"I don't know, but miracles do happen sometimes."

Every six hours I had to give more sedatives to the weiro. Two days later he was able to sit up on the towel, but his head was still nearly upside down, which made him look a bit funny. He had to be fed via crop needle and was losing weight rapidly. Occasionally he would go into convulsions again and needed to be held to protect him from injury.

Two more days later and the weiro was able to sit on a perch and eat a few seeds with his head sideways. Five days on from the accident he could fly short distances and was able to walk and climb around the cage. His owners were delighted. My own pet weiro was now missing his newfound friend, even though he was a bit jealous of him at times.

It pays to persevere as long as the patient isn't suffering too much. Birds have an amazing ability to recover from injury if given the chance. I will always remember this little darling of a bird!

38

Heartbreak again

Lyn, the vet nurse, rang me from the clinic while I was in the house next to it.

"You have an emergency."

A car had pulled up. An elderly woman approached me. She was very distraught.

"I think Buddy has three broken legs," she sobbed.

A kelpie dog was lying on the floor of the passenger side of the car. One of his back legs was clearly broken at the hock joint and the bone was sticking out with the lower part of the leg hanging from the skin. Buddy looked at me calmly and helplessly. I immediately examined the rest of him and found both of his front paws severely injured with several fractures. I felt a lump in my throat and couldn't keep the tears back.

"The kindest thing would be to put him down," I said with trepidation in my voice.

"He has been a wonderful dog, and I don't want him to suffer," the woman said.

Buddy was a working dog as well and would not be very happy as a cripple even if he could be saved. I gave Buddy a last pat on the head and then injected him with the anaesthetic overdose in his vein where he was lying on the car floor. He quietly passed away and was now free of pain.

I gave his owner a hug. She thanked me for helping Buddy in his last moments and freeing him from pain. She took Buddy home to be buried at the property.

It took me the rest of the morning to recover from the incident. I wondered quietly how paramedics cope with seeing people badly injured in car accidents. At least they don't have to put the people down.

39
Has my cat been poisoned?

It was Sunday, and a young chap called Peter turned up at the surgery with a dead cat. He asked me if I would look at it to establish the cause of death. It was his girlfriend's cat, and he was worried the cat had been killed maliciously by somebody. The cat's name was Bella. About two hours earlier Bella had been sitting happily on the roof of the house. Peter had gone out for a short while. When he came back, he found Bella dead under a tree in the garden. His girlfriend was distraught.

"Her head was twisted in a funny way as if someone had broken her neck," Peter said.

I thought, *how would you go about breaking a cat's neck without getting scratched to death?* I examined Bella's dead body on the surgery table. It was still warm. All her claws were very badly frayed. When a cat gets hit by a vehicle, they grab hold of the bitumen with all four feet and the claws get ripped and frayed. This is usually a telltale sign of a hit by car accident. There was only a tiny mark on her thigh. I turned Bella over. The whole side of her body felt all macerated, and her ribs were broken under the skin, although there wasn't a mark on the fur.

"Bella has been run over by a car," I said. "The wheels must have gone right over her body."

Cats are amazingly resilient; they are said to have "nine lives". How Bella still managed to get back under the tree with such horrific injuries is nothing short of a mystery. She must have bled to death internally.

Peter was very grateful for me having done the post-mortem on a Sunday. At least he and his girlfriend would feel easier knowing the death was caused by an accident and not by malicious intent. He thanked me and took the body with him and left.

I had a quiet afternoon, what was left of it.

40

A natural brew for sick sheep

In Western Australia they have a lot of sheep. Katanning is in the heart of the sheep country. Many families have made a lot of money out of wool. As a vet in Katanning I used to see a few valuable rams and even ewes, and sometimes they were just valuable as pets.

One woman had a funny-looking, malformed pet sheep that reminded me of a thalidomide-affected human. The sheep had four very stumpy, short legs with crooked joints. It looked a bit like a dachshund with wool. It had difficulty trying to get around on the malformed legs. The owner brought it in because it had developed arthritis in its joints. She loved her pet, which she had reared since a baby lamb, and wouldn't dream of having it put down.

Often sheep were presented to me because they had eaten

too much grain, which can be very crippling if not lethal to a sheep. One client had imported a fairly unusual breed of sheep named Texels from South Australia. The Texel is a funny little thickset sheep bred for its meat. The wool is very coarse and not of any importance. The new owners had one ram and twenty ewes trucked over from South Australia to Western Australia. Then they made the cardinal mistake of spoiling the animals by giving them grain. The ram and a ewe got desperately ill soon after arrival to their new home and died on the way in to the surgery. I suspected grain poisoning and confirmed it with a necropsy. I explained to the owners how important it was that they treated the remaining sheep urgently and took them off the grain all together.

Unfortunately, by the time a sheep shows sign of grain poisoning a lot of damage has already been done, and the animals often die days later after a lingering illness. The grain produces a lot of acid inside the rumen, the second stomach. The newly imported Texels kept on dying no matter what treatment they were given. One late afternoon the owners called me out in desperation to get the remaining ones treated with fluids and electrolytes via stomach tube. The three of us worked for four hours catching and sitting the stubborn Texels on their bottoms so that I could pass a plastic tube down to their stomach. They kept refusing to cooperate by kicking and by chewing on the tube. A couple of the sheep were so stubborn that we had to let them go since they got too stressed by the procedure. I returned home after an hour's drive in the dark late at night, full of bruises and covered in electrolytes.

The Texels still kept on dying, and eventually there were only six left. They still weren't eating, and I suggested that they should be drenched with the contents from the rumen of healthy sheep. The rumen is the second of a sheep's four stomachs. They contain all the little microbes that break down the fibrous food that sheep live on. These microbes had been killed by the acid from the grain. Without these little helpers the sheep would literally starve.

The local sheep abattoir was very helpful. They let us have a nice big bucket of very smelly rumen contents from some recently slaughtered sheep. The next job we had to do was to strain off the solids. I found some old fly screen netting lying around and held it over a bucket while the solid contents were poured into it. With a bit of squeezing of the gauze we got a nice brown pongy liquid just right to go down a stomach tube.

The same battle took place as that dark long night a couple of weeks earlier, with kicking and wriggling Texels. Only this time I drenched them in the back of a truck under a shade tree on a nice sunny day. Hopefully this natural, living brew would get the Texels' digestive system going again after a prolonged period of anorexia.

No more of the Texels died after this last treatment. They were soon back to their normal selves. The smelly, yucky natural brew did the trick!

41

The things vets have to do

ONE TIME ONE OF OUR most valued sheep clients had left a ram in the horse box at the surgery to have its knee attended to. Normally I used to treat similar cases in the back of the owner's truck with the owner restraining the ram as I did what had to be done. This morning I had been out, and when I returned to the surgery there was this huge woolly beast with huge cork-screw horns, strutting around the horsebox with its head held high in the air.

"Now how are we going to catch that?" I said to Lyn, my assistant, as we both gazed at the wild-looking animal.

"I don't know," she replied apprehensively.

"You are bigger than me, you can do it," I said hopefully.

"No, I'm scared of male sheep since I was rouseabouting once and this big wether went for me and sent me flying to the floor. I don't trust the buggers."

"Maybe we can corner him in behind the gate and attack him from behind?" I said.

"Yeah, but when they see a gap next to you they don't realise that even if their bodies may fit through this little gap their horns are this much wider and they catch you in the legs as they dash past and it hurts like hell!"

Lyn was demonstrating the difference between the width of a ram's body and its horns by holding out her hands at the appropriate distances, not without a bit of exaggeration.

"I believe you," I said. "How about lassoing him over the horns? I used to lasso horses. It is fun."

I got out a thick rope that was used as a leg rope for horses and I threw it at the ram. The ram quickly dodged the noose and took off past the both of us and through the gate into the shed. The veterinary vehicle was parked in this shed and the ram disappeared behind it.

"Quick! Block the other side so I can get him as he comes past me!" I sung out to Lyn.

The ram came flying along the side of the car and I managed to slip the rope over his curled horns. Now I had seventy kilograms of angry ram at the end of the rope. His swollen knee didn't seem to slow him down at all.

"Help me hold him until I can get the rope around the bull bar of the car," I shouted.

The ram was caught but banged heavily into the already old and battered vet car as he struggled to get free. I grabbed him by the horns and twisted his head, trying to tip him off his feet.

"Grab his back legs so he falls over!"

Lyn got both the ram's back legs, so he was now sitting

helplessly on his rear end. She tied the two back legs and one front leg together with a piece of rope.

After all this I could at last treat the ram's swollen but painless knee and bandage it up and he was ready to let go back into the horse box after just a few minutes.

42

Don't panic! You can do it!

BRUCELLOSIS IN SHEEP IS A venereal disease that causes infertility in rams. There was a voluntary scheme in Western Australia of trying to eradicate the disease by blood testing all rams on partaking farms and culling animals that tested positive. I was called upon to blood test between fifty and two hundred rams in one visit. I had never taken blood from any kind of sheep before and now I had to do two hundred at once!

There were basically only two alternatives to take the blood: the jugular vein in the neck or the cephalic vein on the foreleg. I also had to palpate every ram's testicles for signs of disease as part of the scheme. One person had to mark all the blood samples while another caught the rams and tipped them over so they were presented to me sitting on their butts with all four feet in the air.

The farm with the two hundred rams was well over an hour's drive from the surgery in Katanning. I had arranged to be there by 7 am. The farmer and his wife were drafting many separate mobs of rams into the shearing shed as I arrived.

The rams varied in age and size, but the biggest ones would have been close to eighty kilograms in weight. I wondered quietly what kind of back the farmer must have to be able to manhandle all two hundred animals in one day! I was glad I only had to handle the needles, even if I did end up with a few needle stabs at the end of the job.

Shearing sheds, mostly raised off the ground, have this fantastic flooring that allows for the sheep manure – which is in the form of small pellets – to fall between the narrow slats to the space below. But this same design also allows for any other reasonably small items such as pens and syringes to be hopelessly lost if by any chance they are dropped or kicked out of your hand by an uncooperative sheep.

We were all set up to start, with a forty-four-gallon drum serving very well as a table for the samples and so on. The farmer grabbed a big woolly ram for me to start on.

"I'll use the jugular," I said to him as I parted the thick wool on the neck of the nearly upside-down sheep, trying to look for the jugular groove. It was impossible to see anything but wool, so I tried to feel for the deep groove on either side of the neck in which the jugular vein was supposed to lie. With the thumb of my left hand pressing into the groove to try and raise the vein I tentatively stabbed the patient ram repeatedly above my thumb where I knew the vein must be but to no avail. It was like trying to get blood out of a stone.

"Let's try the foreleg," I said, still full of hope.

I showed the farmer how to hold the animal's foreleg so that its cephalic vein would fill up. These British-breed rams had very woolly legs as well as necks and no vein was to be found on the leg either. In desperation the farmer dragged the ram to a set of over-head shears and shore the wool off the leg. In the half-dark of the shed it was hard to see anything at the best of times.

I soon gave up on the leg and decided to go full bore at the jugular. After twenty minutes I still couldn't get any blood.

It is only practice, I told myself in my head. *You know there is a huge vein in the neck. Don't worry that the farmer thinks you are hopeless. You know you can do it really well if you don't panic.*

"Try another sheep," I said, full of hope. "That one must have been a hard one."

I parted the wool on this second one, felt for the groove, put my thumb deeply into it, stabbed the needle above my thumb and: Voila! Success! Once I realised that positioning the animal's head a certain way made all the difference, all the rest of the rams went like a song. We had them done in less than half a day including tea break.

That goes to show you the truth in the old adage that practice makes perfect. And don't panic!

43

A sad day: three euthanasias

BEING A VET CAN SOMETIMES be very sad and stressful, especially when you have to put people's beloved pets down for different reasons. One time we had a particularly sad day.

First thing at 8 am, a man arrived who had phoned me the night before nearly choking on tears as he explained that his dog had to be put down because it had bitten someone. The man broke down in tears again as he approached me outside the surgery.

"I was all right until I got here," he said. "Remember Scout? You got a grass seed out of his ear last time he was here. You had to put a muzzle on him and sedate him."

Scout was a big brown kelpie and he didn't like vets, so he growled when I approached him in the back of the utility.

"I'll put the muzzle on him so you can handle him," his distressed owner said.

While this was going on the town's optometrist had come in with Princess, one of his three Siamese cats. Princess was very sick, he told Lyn, and she said he could leave the cat for me to have a look at when I got a chance.

Next, Lyn and I had to put Scout to sleep. Lyn had to hold the dog and bring up the vein on his right foreleg. He growled viciously and I was glad he had a muzzle on. Ten seconds after I had given the lethal injection in the vein, he peacefully went to sleep forever, and we carried his lifeless body out to his distressed owner.

After Scout's owner had left, I took a look at the sick cat. The nice little Siamese was more than sick. Princess was moribund and on her last legs. So I had to ring and tell the cat's owner the sad news that there was no hope Princess would get better and that she needed to be put to sleep. Then he cried as well. I asked him if he wanted to be present at the euthanasia, but he said he would rather not and for me to go ahead. Fifteen minutes later he turned up at the surgery with tears in his eyes to take Princess' body home for burial in the garden. I was handing out tissues all morning it seemed.

And then to top things off, later in the day yet another person turned up with an old dog with a broken leg.

"We have spent that much money on him already. He had a broken leg before and you fixed it. He is not a very good sheep dog so if it is going to cost a lot I would rather you put him down."

Since it was going to cost several hundred dollars to repair the old dog's leg, we were faced with the option of putting down the third animal for the day. At least the last person didn't seem to be too worried about the sad fate of his dog and there were no tears this time. But looks can be deceiving.

44

The joys of being a large-animal vet

It had been a quiet week at the Katanning surgery. The days were moseying along and the vet nurse went home at three o'clock every afternoon, but I had to keep shop until six o'clock five days a week regardless. It got a bit boring all on my lonesome.

But don't fear! After sitting and wishing something would happen all day, at last I closed the clinic at six and walked over to the house to start making tea for me and a friend I had invited over. We no sooner got started eating the first mouthful of steak when the phone rang.

"I have a cow that can't calve," said a concerned voice on the phone.

"I just found her standing there with a dead calf hanging

down from her behind nearly to the ground," the man continued. "She's a heifer on her first calf."

After getting some more information I said I would come out shortly. The farmer would wait for me at the highway turnoff to his property.

I had lost my appetite but gulped down most of the now-cold dinner. I apologised to my visitor that I had to leave so soon.

It was dark and cold and drizzling with rain as I drove out to this poor cow in labour. After a twenty-minute drive I spotted a stationary car with headlights on at a side road. I pulled off the road and stopped behind the car, waiting for it to start leading me to the property with the cow. The car took off in the distance on a slippery dirt road and I was flat out keeping up in the old Volvo I was driving. The Volvo had a worn-out windscreen that scattered the light in all directions when it got wet, so I had difficulty seeing the road. More so after the car ahead increased the gap between us and I couldn't follow in its light beam anymore.

Eventually we reached the gate into the paddocks. It proved to be a long drive over gullies and banks and slippery wet patches. The old Volvo did not have four-wheel drive.

The heifer was sitting quietly under a tree, with a huge calf still stuck by its hips, its lifeless body trailing behind her on the ground. The heifer was huge herself, a cross between a Murray Grey and a Hereford. I walked over in the torchlight and bent down and grabbed a leg of the carcass. I tried to pull out the rest of the dead, swollen calf as the heifer was lying there. She got up and tried to get away from me. As she got up the farmer put his arms around her neck to stop her from running off. The animal's head was nearly as big as the farmer himself!

It didn't take much to get the lifeless calf out. Once the heifer was up, the weight of the carcass made it just about fall out. The poor heifer nearly had a prolapse of the uterus immediately afterwards. After checking her over, I decided that she would be OK. She walked off in the night to lie down.

After all this I paused and took in the peaceful cool night with relief. It felt good to have managed to help the poor animal. It had stopped raining and the moonlight was penetrating the clouds, so it was quite light. Everything was perfectly still. The rest of the cattle in the paddock came over to investigate the fate of their mate. They all lined up side by side, with their heads facing the heifer that was now lying exhausted on the ground.

The farmer took me halfway back to the road through the paddocks again. I found my way back home the rest of the way. It hadn't been too hard of a job, at least no need for a caesarean in the night.

I got back home 9 pm. *Ahh! A lovely hot bath to soak in*, I thought. I had not been able to wash off any of the blood and mess yet, because there had been no water available on site and I never carried any in the vehicle. I probably should in the future!

I had barely got my cold feet and legs warmed up in the nice warm water when the phone rang again. I got out of the bath onto the cold concrete floor and answered the phone shivering with cold and with water dripping off my legs. It was the same farmer again.

"You're not going to like me for this," he said hesitantly. "I've just found another cow in trouble."

The farmer explained to me that after I had left, he had gone looking for a missing cow. He had found the cow in a creek with a calf stuck in her birth canal.

"I'll be right out," I said. I wiped off my legs and got back into my dirty clothes, hopped in the car and left.

This other cow proved to be cast nearly upside down, halfway down a muddy creek bank. She had actually managed to calve in this awkward position by the time we got back to her. The calf was sitting on top of the bank, resting. I felt immense relief at not having to pull a calf out in this slippery position. Luckily the moon was still out so I could see something!

"We need to turn the cow over so she can get her feet under her," I said.

I had some ropes with me, and we slung one rope around the bottom hind leg and another around the front leg. It was tricky to find any solid footing in the dark night to give a good pull on the ropes. Luckily the ropes were long enough so we could stand on the grassy bank. Then it was only a matter of rolling the cow right over and onto her feet. She soon found her calf and attended to it by licking it all over.

This had been an eventful night, but I loved every minute of it. To be able to help these wonderful placid creatures with their wet noses and sweet-smelling breath can only be described as one of life's most satisfying experiences. I returned home that night to finish my now not-so-hot bath. I went to bed around midnight for a very nice and well-deserved rest.

45

Pigs, dogs and corncobs

At Mitchell Vet Hospital in Katanning we used to see an array of animals, anything from horses and cows to sheep and rabbits, ferrets, chooks and wildlife. One day a man phoned about his pig.

"I've got a pig with mastitis," the voice at the other end said.

"What makes you think that?" I asked.

"She's lying on her belly, and she won't feed the piglets."

"How old are the piglets and how many are there?" I asked, trying to get a picture of the situation.

"She had ten last Thursday, but she laid on a couple, so there are eight left. It's mastitis, isn't it?"

"Sounds like it could be. Do you want me to check her out?"

"Just as well. My wife has been bottle feeding the little ones a couple of times. It's a lot of mucking around."

"Have you got a big piggery or just a few?"

"Just a couple of sows."

I enjoyed the prospect of a new challenge and happily drove out to the farm.

The owner of the pigs had on one occasion in the past brought in his sick dog one evening. The dog had been vomiting for a few days and looked very sad and tucked up. I put the dog on a drip for the night. In the morning I found a tail-wagging dog in the hospital cage, looking nothing like the night before. On the cage floor was a strange object. I picked it up and realised it was part of a corn cob! The dog must have eaten it days before and since it was indigestible it had remained in the stomach, causing gastritis. Luckily it had not passed on into the intestines where it would have caused a serious blockage. The dog had eventually managed to vomit the corncob up after trying for days unsuccessfully.

I was now walking down the paddock together with the pig's owner towards some low-set tin sheds. Tiger, the corncob dog, came along happily. He must have remembered me! The tin sheds looked like the remnants of a typical old-fashioned Australian farm. Old corrugated iron sheds everywhere, of all shapes and sizes. The wind was tearing into bits of flapping iron, making a regular squeaking and banging noise. Adding to the sound was the rattle of an old windmill aimlessly spinning around out of control, no longer pumping any water. The wide, flat wheat fields around the district provided little resistance to the wind that always seemed to blow in this part of the world. To try and slow the demise of the shed roofs caused by the wind, stones and logs had been put on top to hold the sheets of rusty corrugated iron down.

The sow and her piglets lived in a pen made of old bits of

timber driven into the ground and held together with wire. They had a little tin hut to go into out of the weather. The sow was lying in a deep puddle of mud on her belly, so the piglets had no chance of getting to her nipples.

"This is where she stays all day apart from when she is eating her feed," the farmer said. "She won't let the piglets drink at all."

She was a fair-sized sow, and I wondered how I would be able to take her temperature. I had brought a rope to snare her snout with, but the problem was there was nowhere to tie her to that was strong enough.

"Have you got a pig race or a small space where we can put her?" I said to the farmer.

"No, nothing like that."

"If you've got a sheet of tin or something we can try and corner her so I can examine her," I said hopefully.

The farmer found an old gate made of steel piping with wire netting across. The trouble was the netting only covered three-quarters of the gate. We then both tried to encourage the big sow into a corner of the pen. The farmer tried to push the gate across the corner. The sow let out a succession of aggressive grunts and forced herself through the missing wire part. She hurriedly headed for the deep mud part of the pen. The bewildered piglets ran everywhere squealing. One poor little piglet got knocked down and run over by its somewhat upset mother. When the sow was approached by the farmer again, she grunted wildly and advanced with open mouth, head held high. The farmer put his boot up in her face to try and keep her off. The angry sow grabbed hold of the boot; he lost his footing and fell backwards in the mud.

"I won't worry about examining her," I said, feeling a bit

embarrassed. The farmer rose from the mud and brushed off the dirt from his clothes.

"I'll just give her an antibiotic needle."

That was easier said than done. I didn't want my leg bitten by a stirred-up sow, so I tried to needle her over the fence. But every time I got near her with the needle she quickly moved out of reach.

"Let's see if we can get her into her shelter and I'll try and stab her in there," I said hopefully.

After several unsuccessful attempts I managed to give the sow half of the injection. She didn't appreciate the feel of the needle and broke out of the pig shelter. I climbed back and forth across the pig pen half a dozen times and eventually managed to deliver the remaining dose on the run into the sow's thick hide.

Two hours later I headed back to the clinic. It had been an interesting day to say the least.

46

A hypochondriac horse, or owner?

WHEN DEALING WITH PEOPLE YOU get all kinds. That makes the job more interesting I suppose! Some people are very demanding and think their problem is the only one that counts.

I was busy one Friday afternoon with a dog under anaesthetic on the surgery table. Lyn, my vet nurse, answered the phone. She came running in to me.

"It's Jane Simpson and she wants to know if you can put her horse down now!"

Jane came from a very well-off farming family and was in her early twenties. She had always got what she wanted and was a very demanding client. She had a chestnut riding mare that was only six years old, and she had spent a small fortune on it in vet bills already. The mare had had everything under the sun wrong with it. It had even been taken to the university equine hospital for very expensive abdominal surgery for colic.

A week earlier, Jane had phoned me about her horse again.

"Have you got some selenium supplement I can give my mare? I've had the chiropractor to her, and he thinks she may need some selenium."

Selenium is a trace mineral that is very toxic if used indiscriminately.

"What's the problem with your mare now?" I asked.

"She won't use her hind legs properly. She won't round herself up when I collect her. The chiropractor says she is out in the back."

I was starting to wonder if it wasn't Jane herself that had a problem. Maybe she was looking for problems in her horse. Munchausen syndrome? Or maybe she had a hypochondriac horse?

"Why don't you ride your other two horses and turn your mare out on pasture for six months. Time is a wonderful healer a lot of the time," I explained.

"I might just do that." Jane sounded painfully desperate. "Thanks for the advice anyway," she said.

When Jane phoned me this time a week later, pleading to have her horse put down, I shook my head in disbelief. I phoned Jane back as soon as I was free in less than ten minutes. Her boyfriend answered:

"It is all right, we don't need you now. We have made other arrangements with another vet to have her put down."

I was shocked. Last time I saw the beautiful mare it was perfectly happy, and I couldn't find much wrong with it.

"Why does she want the horse put down?" I asked.

"Oh, we have had several experts look at the horse. It has structural problems and is in a lot of pain."

So instead of showing a bit of patience and let nature do its own work, Jane hysterically wanted to be rid of the whole worry by ending the beautiful mare's life. Some people are hard to work out.

47

Max and the mad cat

Not only do vets have to handle all sorts of people – they also have to handle all sorts of animals. Of all animals, the humble pussycat can prove to be a challenge. These often softly purring balls of fluff also have a razor-sharp set of teeth and an arsenal of needle-sharp claws on all four feet. They also have an uncanny ability to be able to reach just about anywhere and have lightning-fast reflexes. So if your purring creature metamorphoses into a spitting and hissing little devil, you will have to get kitted up in elbow-length leather gloves if you need to become intimate for medication purposes. Many cats hate coming to the vet, mostly by car, and so can be somewhat sullen on arrival.

One day a man we called "Max A Million" came into the surgery. He was concerned about his cat that had been sneezing and snuffling for some weeks.

"I can't catch him to bring him in. He's a very wild cat. I don't know how I'm going to get him in. Can I borrow a cat cage?"

"Sure. It sounds as if the cat needs some attention," I replied.

"But he hates coming here. I don't want to upset him. What do you think is wrong with him? Can it be cured?"

People often expect the vet to diagnose an animal from a mental picture. And then they want you to tell them they already have the remedy in their home.

"He could have cat flu or maybe just a bad cold. He may also have feline leukaemia. We need to do a blood test to find out," I explained.

"Oh, that sounds pretty bad. I was prepared for the worst. He is ten years old so he's not young anymore. Do you think it is feline leuk … emia or whatever?"

"It is not unlikely. But don't let us think the worst before I can have a look at the cat. It may not be anything serious at all."

"So when can I bring him in if I can catch him? He's that wild. He'll claw you to death if you try to catch him. What times are you open? I still don't know how I can get him in here. He will never forgive me. But I suppose it is for his own good," Max said.

I thought, *Why does he bother with a cat that is so unfriendly?*

"I can give you some sedative tablets that you can mix in some milk or food. Try to con him into eating some drugged food. That will make him travel better. They take up to an hour to work," I informed Max.

"I think I'll try and bring him in. I am prepared for the worst when you find out what is wrong with him. It's a real worry. I don't want to give him any drugs. He would not take them anyway."

Three days later Max returned with a black cat in the cat cage.

"I don't know how you'll get him out of the cage. He'll take off or try and claw you to death if you try to touch him. He'd kill you if he could. And by the way please don't phone me about the results of the test. I will come in on Thursday to find out. I can't bear to go around waiting for that fateful phone call."

After Max had left Lyn got the big leather gloves ready for this apparently dreadful animal. We carried Max's cat into the surgery room in the cage he had arrived in. So far, he hadn't been hissing or spitting anywhere. We closed all the doors in case he should manage to get away from us. I drew up a sedative into a syringe to be ready for the exciting moment when this monster would meet his master.

"All right, are you ready with the gloves? I am going to open the cage," I said to Lyn. We both waited in tense suspense.

Miaaaow! A black face appeared from the depths of the cage.

"This cat doesn't exactly appear wild to me," I said to Lyn. "And listen! He's purring!"

The black cat strutted out onto the table with a confident look on his face. I began to stroke him on the head, to which he avidly responded by arching his back against my hand.

"How wild and dangerous is this?!" both Lyn and I said in chorus.

After playing with the much-misunderstood pussycat for a while, I went on to examine him with ease. He was a big overweight animal with the only overt sign of a problem being a snuffly nose. He even let us take a blood sample without much trouble.

So much for that. Even if this cat was feeling sick at the time, it didn't seem possible that he had ever been the monster his owner had portrayed him to be.

48

You try, and sometimes you fail

I had worked for over a year in Katanning and not seen any snakebite cases, then we had three cases in less than a week! The two first cases were dogs that never made it alive to the surgery. One had been bitten by a tiger snake and was dead within two hours.

The one patient that did make it to the surgery alive – the first snakebite case I ever saw – was the least typical one could ever expect. We had had some unseasonably warm autumn weather, and the snakes must have come out of hibernation for a while. The patient, a six-month-old Staffy, had been out in the paddock with its owner and had "taken a fit" as the owner put it.

"My dog has just taken a fit." The man on the phone sounded very casual. "What can I do about it?"

From his casual description I gathered that it couldn't be very serious or urgent.

"It would be best if you could bring him in," I explained.

I had gotten prepared two hours earlier for a snake bite in another dog, reading up all about it and getting the antivenene ready. But that dog had, sadly, died on the way. I didn't for one moment think that the "fitting" dog about to arrive would be a snake bite. It didn't seem serious enough, going by the owner. I expected one of those mysterious "puppy fits" that I had seen on several occasions that seem to go away in a couple of hours, often with no treatment needed at all.

Bruno arrived in the arms of his previously casual-sounding owner. The dog was very distressed and struggled to breathe. His mucous membranes were absolutely white! That is very serious indeed and indicates that the animal is in deep shock and the circulatory system is failing. Bruno was unable to stand up and reacted violently to being touched. For a moment I thought, *strychnine bait*, because this is how a dog reacts that has eaten strychnine. Then the dog coughed up a pink froth. This made me almost convinced that the dog had been bitten by a snake.

"It's a snake bite," I said while searching for bite marks on Bruno's head and legs. Then I found two small red puncture marks on the back of the dog's foreleg.

"Here you go," I said to the owner. "This is where he was bitten. I have got brown snake antivenene, but it won't do any good if it was a tiger snake that bit him. And it is very expensive. Do you still want to go ahead with treatment with brown snake antivenene just in case it will work?"

The owner said to go ahead, so I put the extremely stressed

dog on an intravenous drip and premedicated it for shock and then slowly gave it the antivenene via the drip line straight into the blood stream. The dog seemed to improve slightly with a sedative as well as the antivenene. I put him in a cage for observation for the rest of the day.

Towards the evening Bruno was still having difficulty breathing and was sitting on his haunches to facilitate expansion of the lungs. He didn't look much better than before. He struggled through the night and the next day until about 4 pm.

Then he started throwing fits again in the cage. I rushed to try and calm him down but as soon as he was touched his whole body went into a violent spasm with all four legs thrown into extension and head thrown back. I decided the best for him was to put him under a long-acting intravenous anaesthetic. It would relax his body and prevent further fits. It would also make him unconscious so he wouldn't have to feel any suffering. And I could give him oxygen straight into his lungs via a tube into the windpipe.

Bruno spent thirty-six hours in an induced coma, but his breathing became more and more laboured and shallow. His gum colour now stayed bluish even when he was breathing straight oxygen. I didn't hold much hope for him at this stage. But he was still peaceful, and I couldn't bear to put him down after all this. However, at eleven that evening he died.

The autopsy showed that Bruno's lungs had become clogged up with clotted blood to such an extent that practically no blood could get through at all. And all the fine airways were full of froth caused by the congestion, leading to a secondary drowning as well.

Snake venom has many components. One component

causes paralysis of the muscles. Another causes the blood to clot inside the small arteries. My conclusion is that the snake venom caused Bruno's blood to clot in his lungs soon after being bitten. This led to a massive congestion of the lungs that just got worse and worse until it eventually prevented enough blood from getting through to pick up oxygen to sustain life. This caused him to virtually suffocate to death. He never suffered because he was in a coma until death.

Bruno's owner was devastated at the news. I did my best but sometimes no matter what you do, you will fail. That is the hard part of being a vet.

49

Sadly, bad accidents do happen

Before I became a vet, I used to handle a lot of young unbroken horses when I worked as a cattle stud manager in the early eighties. I bred some working horses of my own and handled them from a day old. That way there was less risk of the horse or handler getting hurt. It was very easy to inadvertently overbalance an unhandled horse the first time he was caught with a rope. Often they would rear up in the air and come down with a crash if you didn't release the pull on the neck rope in time before they reared up too high. With a small foal you could prevent the head from hitting the ground if they did rear over by holding the rope short as they came down. But with a two-year-old it is very dangerous for the horse if he comes down backwards from rearing high in the air on his back legs.

One sunny Queensland day many years ago, I was watching an old horseman by the name of Jack handle a couple of thoroughbred yearlings in a typical Australian bush yard made of ironbark rails. Needless to say, the yards weren't ideal to handle yearlings in. The yard was square instead of round. This tended to encourage the horse to try and hide its head in the corners and turn the tail to the handler.

In a round yard a horse can be made to run in a circle and a rope can be thrown from behind the moving horse to catch it around the neck. If you throw the rope in front of the horse thinking the horse will run through the loop, you will be surprised at the agility by which the horse manages to quickly duck its head to avoid getting caught by the loop.

Jack was in his seventies and had handled and broken in horses all his life. The bay thoroughbred colt in the yard had never been touched by a human hand and had never had a rope around his neck before. He was about fourteen months old and in good paddock condition. He wasn't an unduly nervy colt but the separation from his mates for the first time in his short life made him very upset. His whole body vibrated as he whinnied out loudly when he saw his mates gallop back down the paddock.

It is very traumatic for a horse to be separated from his equine friends, but it is a necessary part of his education. Horses are herd animals and rely on each other's ears and eyes for safety from attack from large carnivores. They feel very vulnerable when left separated from other equines. Little do they realise that their greatest danger comes from their own ability to injure themselves, not from any horse-eating beasts.

The first thing to do to tame this wild colt was to get a rope around his neck. I am not saying that it was ideal to throw a rope at a frightened horse, but this was the way Jack caught his horses. Jack swung the lasso loop towards the frightened colt, who was facing the gate in the bottom corner of the yard. The noose found its target first up and slid over the face of the colt. Jack sent a ripple along the rope to make the loop fall down over the muzzle and end up low around the colt's neck. The colt was dumbfounded and didn't know that he was caught or what was to follow. He was still facing the corner away from Jack at the end of the rope.

The idea with the rope is not to try and hang on to the much stronger horse but to give little tugs on it at the right time. The right time is when the handler has the advantage of leverage against the horse. The correct leverage is gained when the horse's body is at right angles to the rope. This is where the round yard comes in handy. There aren't any corners for the horse to get out of position as easily.

Jack's colt was definitely not in the correct position to be controlled by the rope. The colt would first have to be eased out of the corner before he was given his first pull on the noose around his neck. Jack was not an ill-tempered man, but he tended to be a bit impatient. He tapped the colt on the rump with his stock whip and the colt spun around the opposite way and got the rope tangled between his front legs.

After untangling the rope Jack eventually got the colt into position for a control pull low on the rope. The colt was taken by surprise, and his front feet and shoulders left the ground to spin around with the head in response to the pull and the horse ended up facing the handler for a split second. Every time the colt tried to turn away from Jack in the centre of the yard, he got a short pull on the neck rope to spin his front end in facing the centre again. And every time he faced the handler he got slack on the rope as a reward.

Then just as things looked as if they were going according to plan, the colt got smart and tried to wheel away from the annoying rope. Jack responded a bit too slowly and gave a pull on the rope as the horse was out of position. The colt reared up against the rope in an instant. The pull on the rope caused the colt to overbalance while high in the air on his back legs. He came down heavily on his side and, with a thud, hit his neck hard on the hard ground.

The colt got up quickly, looking a bit disoriented but seemingly unharmed. Jack decided that the colt had had enough for the day and let him go back down the paddock with his mates. He trotted away happily.

The next day when the horses were run into the yards again the bay colt was nowhere to be seen. After looking around the horse paddock, he was sadly found on his side unable to move his legs or body at all. He was humanely destroyed on the spot.

I did a post-mortem on the colt's neck later. The second vertebra from the head had split in half from the heavy fall. The colt had unsuspectedly run out the yard the previous day with a broken neck. Later on, the swelling and bleeding into the spinal cord made him totally paralysed.

50

When you can't trust the owner's story

AN INCIDENT SOMEWHAT SIMILAR TO the colt with the broken neck happened with a dog that was presented to me when I worked in Katanning, this time as a vet.

Bing was a forty-kilogram kelpie that used to work with his owner in the sheep yards in Katanning on sale days once a week. One day while working in the sale yards his owner noticed that the dog appeared hunched up as if in pain. The owner suspected the dog of having eaten something that had given him a belly ache.

"Is there any possibility that the dog could have fallen off a ramp or gotten kicked by something?" I asked Bing's owner on arrival.

"Not a chance, I have been working with the dog all morning. He has definitely not had an accident of any kind."

Unfortunately, in my earlier veterinary career I used to put too much emphasis on the owner's account of what had happened. I have come to realise later that people don't want to think that their pet was ill because of their owner's negligence. They would often aggressively deny that they had anything to do with their pet's ill fortune.

I had an extremely busy day when Bing was admitted, so he was given a quick overhaul and put in a cage for observation and maybe x-rays later. He didn't seem unduly distressed on arrival. He was able to stand up and walk without assistance.

Later that afternoon I decided to x-ray Bing's abdomen, which seemed very tucked up and sore. The vet nurse and I carried the very heavy dog across the surgery to the low x-ray table in the far corner. The x-rays didn't show anything abnormal as far as I could make out. Our equipment wasn't the best and it was somewhat difficult to get good x-rays of such a big dog.

The next day Bing seemed to be unable to stand and even though his reflexes seemed normal, I seriously suspected that he had a spinal injury. It was the weekend, and I had to call in the vet nurse to help me carry the big dog to the x-ray table again. We x-rayed the entire spine, which took a bit of doing since we only had small films suited for smaller animals than Bing. I could not see anything abnormal on these films either.

I phoned Bing's owner and emphasised that the dog must have sustained a fall because he was now a quadriplegic from spinal injury with little hope of recovery. The owner still was not convinced and wanted to see proof on an x-ray. I told him that I had x-rayed the dog's spine but because of the dog's size, more sophisticated equipment and maybe a myelogram was needed to get a diagnostic film. To do a myelogram you have to inject a contrast agent into the spinal canal to see if the spinal cord has any lesions. I suggested a referral to the university in Perth but pointed out that the dog's chances of recovery were next to nil. The owner still wanted to take Bing to Perth for more x-rays.

The next day I was informed that Bing had been put to sleep at the university clinic in Perth. X-rays of his neck had confirmed a fracture of the second vertebra from the head.

Since this incident and many others later on, I tend to consider the information given to me by the owner of an injured pet with a pinch of salt. Nowadays I look at the animal's symptoms first and then consider the owner's story to see if it makes sense.

51

Doubting female vets again?

I WENT TO SEE A HORSE that belonged to Mr Pickford. He first asked me on the phone who I was and if I was a *horse vet*. I told him that indeed I was and could he explain what was ailing the horse.

"He has swollen front legs and refuses to walk."

"Is he on a lush green paddock?" I asked. The answer was affirmative.

"Well, he could be foundered," I said, thinking of the last horse that I had seen recently. "Did you want me to come out and examine him?"

Mr Pickford said he wanted the horse seen to, so I loaded up the car in a bit of a hurry and went on my way.

At my destination I was, to my surprise, met by John Haddon, a well-known and very critical horse client of the

Katanning vet clinic. It was obvious that John was a good friend of Mr Pickford's.

At the stables I introduced myself to Mr Pickford.

"Ah so you are the specialist horse vet. Let's see how good you are and if you can tell what's wrong with my horse," he said smugly.

In the dark of the stable stood a giant-sized, gentle bay gelding in a rather lean condition.

"Has he had anything but green feed, any grain?"

"No. But he seems to have an appetite. He's eaten the chaff we just gave him."

"When did you first notice anything wrong?"

"Today. But I haven't seen him for a week. He was OK a week ago."

I walked up and patted the gentle giant.

"Is he always this quiet?" I asked, trying my best to sound knowledgeable.

"My horses are all this well behaved. But what do you think is wrong with him?" Both Mr Pickford and John were now ready to criticise every move I did.

"I'll know when I have examined him. Has he had any tetanus shots?" I asked while I was taking the gelding's temperature via the rectum.

"Do you think he has tetanus now?"

"No, I am just asking." I checked the thermometer and noticed the temperature was up. "Has the horse had a runny nose at all?"

"Don't know. Haven't seen him for a week. You sure ask a lot of questions. Have you worked out what's wrong with him yet?"

"I have a fair idea. I will let you know when I have finished the examination." I was checking the pulse in the digital artery down by the fetlock. It was normal. I picked up both the gelding's front feet. He let me have both feet with no sign of pain from standing on only one foot at a time. I only noticed a slight stiffness on bending the horse's knees.

"Can you please lead the horse out onto the gravel?" I asked. A third onlooker had meanwhile materialised onto the scene. He took the lead rope and tried to get the horse to follow him out of the stable.

The gelding was reluctant to walk at first but suppled up after a few strides.

I decided to give the verdict to the horse's impatient owner.

"Your horse has got a virus. He is not feeling his best in general, and his joints are probably aching a bit. The filling in the legs is aggravated from standing around. As he starts to walk a bit the filling will disappear."

"I had noticed that earlier, that after walking the legs got thinner," Mr Pickford said triumphantly, now he had got an answer to his big gnawing question. Then there was a short silence.

"So he is not foundered?" Mr Pickford asked nearly with disappointment in his voice.

"No. It is not founder," I replied reassuringly.

"But will he recover from this virus to be any good after?"

"I can't see why not. But you need to keep him rugged and warm. You can even bandage his legs to keep them warm as well. Feed him some nourishing and palatable food and let him rest. Keep him out of reach of other horses. Here are some anti-inflammatories to reduce his fever and make him feel better. I will give you some antibiotics for him as well."

Mr Pickford seemed satisfied at last. I drove home with a sense of triumph. I had put him in his place.

A week later the horse was back to his normal self.

Luckily this doubt and lack of faith in female vets is not very common these days. I think that some guys still have difficulty accepting that some women can be smarter than the guy himself.

52

Rocket the hyper kelpie in pain

ROCKET WAS A HYPERACTIVE KELPIE dog that was kept as a house pet. He was a very friendly dog but was always "on the go". He didn't know what relaxing meant. His owners rang me one night after hours and were concerned about Rocket's sudden change in behaviour. He had started to lick himself frantically. The owners thought that he might have gotten some chemical on himself that caused irritation. I said they'd better bring Rocket down straight away for a check-up.

In the consulting room Rocket seemed delighted to see the vet! He licked my hand briefly and then settled onto the floor and started to lick his forelegs incessantly. Then he went to lick the rear end a bit but mainly concentrated on the forelegs.

I started with the usual systematic routine examination checking heart, lungs, mucous membranes, pupils and temperature. Rocket's skin seemed normal, with no signs of inflammation or injury. He had not had any vomiting or diarrhoea. He seemed bright and normal apart from his licking.

Next, I started to routinely palpate or feel his whole body. I checked both his front legs, starting at the toes and working up towards the body. They seemed fine. Then I felt all along the top of the spine from the back of the head to the base of the tail. Then I began to feel along the sides of the loin muscles. As I gently worked my way along the loin I found the source of the trouble. Rocket jerked his head around to the painful side, gently snapping at my hand to try and tell me that it hurt there!

When I explained that Rocket must have hurt his back, his owners remembered that a little earlier, the dog had been flying around at a hundred kilometres an hour and had skidded right around onto his back doing a full turn. It was apparent that Rocket was confused by this aching pain he developed in his back and the only way he knew to ease it was to lick himself frantically. After being treated with an anti-inflammatory/painkiller he stopped his frantic behaviour.

I have since found this phenomenon in other dogs in pain. They seem to sometimes express the pain in a variety of peculiar ways. The owners report that the dog's personality has changed all of a sudden. The dog may just seem unnaturally quiet and withdrawn or may howl and run and hide at the other extreme. The way a dog reacts to pain seems to depend on its innate personality.

53

Bluey the ginger cat

Mr and Mrs Bates, a pensioner couple, brought in their beloved ginger cat. It was called Bluey, as redheads in Australia often are for some strange reason. Bluey had been off colour and not eaten for a couple of days.

"Poor old Bluey," Mrs Bates said. "We don't like to see him in pain. He has had a bad tooth; you don't think that is the problem? And he has a bit of a runny eye."

Bluey was crouched up in the wire-topped cat cage looking very sinister indeed, his eyes just thin slits.

"And by the way, he is not a very friendly cat. He bit Dr Thompson last time he was here. He has got a bit of feral in him you see. We've sort of adopted him. He came to our backyard for food, and we've taken a liking to him, the poor old fellow." Mrs Bates looked at her cat with deep empathy.

"The poor old fellow, he is so frightened. He doesn't know it is for his own good," she continued.

I looked around for the leather gloves. All I could find was the impractical lead x-ray gloves. Sometimes you have to use what you can find for the moment. I made sure all doors and windows were closed. With the heavy gloves on I lifted the cage with Bluey in it onto the floor.

"Be careful, he may jump out. He is very quick!" Mrs Bates said with a worried expression on her face.

Bluey reminded me of the calm before the storm. He must have waited for the right moment of action. Ever so carefully I opened the cage lid and slowly tried to stroke the cat with the cumbersome lead gloves. Bluey didn't seem to mind. I tried to get a grasp around his body to lift him out of his cage. He obliged without a struggle, so I lifted him onto the consult table. The moment his feet touched the table he suddenly exploded into action and with a monstrous hiss, he flew onto the floor, where he settled in the corner of the room.

"I told you he was difficult," Mrs Bates said, almost triumphantly.

"I agree," I replied. "I am going to have to sedate him to examine him properly. He will have to stay in overnight. Tomorrow is a holiday, so you won't be able to pick him up until the day after."

"Is he going to be in here all alone tomorrow?"

"I'm afraid so. If you'd rather bring him back after the holiday, I can examine him then."

"That sounds OK."

Thursday morning after the holiday at opening time, there was Mrs Bates again back with Bluey.

"I am so upset. I haven't slept all night for worrying about him. Will you know what's wrong with him after examining him?"

"I'll have a better idea anyway," I replied hopefully.

Bluey didn't prove to be too hard to "needle". All I did was to stick a needle with sedative into him through the cage bars. He only just hissed a bit after the event. He went to sleep OK. On examination I found he was totally jaundiced all over and one kidney was very enlarged.

With little hope of ever medicating Bluey, the best thing would be to put him down. Mrs Bates cried profusely over the phone when I advised her of Bluey's poor state.

"I don't want to murder him!" she cried. She loved Bluey dearly even though he wasn't the most lovable of pets.

"He loves me in his own way," she said.

One of the hardest things I had to do was to inform an owner that their beloved pet is best put down. I got knots in my stomach every time.

I subsequently wrote Mrs Bates a letter of sympathy, assuring her that she had done the right thing in having dear old Bluey put to sleep.

54

A snowstorm and muddy dogs

A COUPLE OF WEEKS AFTER STARTING my new business, Veterinary Home Visits, in southern Tasmania, I was asked to vaccinate eighteen animals in one visit. It was a boarding kennel and stud breeding Alaskan malamutes. The sad story behind this day was that the original owner had died suddenly and unexpectedly from a massive heart attack at the tender age of thirty-five. Some of the family members had come over from a farm in South Australia to sort things out. They were taking three dogs and a cat back with them.

When I left home it was the worst weather I had ever seen since moving to Tasmania; it was snowing heavily. The snow melted as soon as it hit the ground in Kingston where I live, but on the way to the kennel, which lay at a higher altitude, the snow was five centimetres thick on the ground.

I was met by Tracy, a twenty-something girl with short blond hair and dressed in a raincoat. She was the one having to look after the animals.

"Have you got a shed or a place out of the weather where we can check and vaccinate the pups and dogs?" I asked her.

Tracy looked around briefly. "Not really."

I pictured myself trudging around in the muddy kennels picking up wet, dirty pups while the snow iced up my freezing hands. Then I noticed a small aluminium garden shed.

"What about that one?" I asked tentatively, pointing.

"OK, I can put a grooming table in it and we can use that," Tracy happily replied. She left and returned ten minutes later with a rickety small table with foldable legs and a thin plastic top and placed it in the shed. At least it was better than nothing.

The sky darkened even more, and the slushy snowflakes fell heavily onto the ground. I felt the chill into my bones. Tracy went to fetch the first of the malamutes, a beautiful, huge, wolf-like bitch with thick fur and grey-and-white markings. The bitch was soaked in cold mud and Tracy urged her to jump up onto the small, unstable camping table. The large animal leapt onto the table with the smoothness of a big cat without hesitation, as if she had done so hundreds of times before. She looked me straight in the face, a somewhat intimidating experience when your own face is only centimetres away from a large carnivore's!

"She's really gentle," Tracy said with a big smile. The dog started licking my face faithfully.

"I can see that," I replied, somewhat relieved.

Three more big malamutes went onto the table, although we had to lift them all up one by one. They were not able to jump up themselves, or did not want to even after a lot of coaxing. They were all soaked in cold, wet mud and we ended up being covered in mud ourselves. As a vet I have to examine the animals by running my hands along their bodies to feel any unusual lumps and bumps. I also listen to their heart with a stethoscope. Tracy told me that one big male dog, George, suffered from a bad heart. He was only three years old.

"George gets very puffed up when we go anywhere; he has no stamina at all," Tracy said in a sad voice.

I could hear via my stethoscope that George's heart had a very bad murmur on the right side of his chest. This means the heart is not pumping very well and that some blood is running backwards through a leak in the heart valves; it will get worse with time. The heart has to work a lot harder.

A happy-looking black-and-white cat strolled past the shed.

"Her name is Missy," Tracy said fondly.

"Let's grab Missy and vaccinate her now she is here," I said. The pussycat didn't object at all at the unusual attention. She didn't even try to run away when I went to pick her up, contrary to what a lot of my other feline patients do. I started by checking her mouth.

"She has a very bad tooth on this side," I said to Tracy. Missy cooperated just fine with me opening her mouth to see what was going on inside.

"It will need some attention," I informed Tracy.

Tracy next brought over two malamute pups to be vaccinated, one under each arm. One had black-and-white markings. There were nine six-week-old pups in the litter.

"They are all so gorgeous," I said delightedly. "I love working with young puppies, who doesn't?"

The pups were all muddy and smelly, since they all lived in a pen together. Their tummies bulged with food and they all seemed very healthy. I started examining the black-and-white pup.

"Unfortunately this one has a problem with the heart," I said to Tracy after listening to its heart with the stethoscope. "It has a loud murmur on both sides and the front of the chest, and it usually means that the connection between the two sides of the heart hasn't closed off properly at birth. It may close off by itself later, but it is unlikely. The pup will gradually get a lot worse and have to be put down. You can have him ultra-sounded to confirm."

"Can it be fixed?" Tracy asked. She sounded very worried.

"It can be fixed, but it means invasive and tricky open chest surgery and it is very expensive. And there are no guarantees that the pup will survive the surgery," I said.

"Oh well, he is sold to a friend of mine. They sold very cheap, and she will have to decide what to do with him later," Tracy replied matter-of-factly.

Tracy had yet another three Pembroke corgis for me to check and vaccinate. They were also all very sweet-natured and friendly. Of course, none of them could jump onto the table with their short stumpy legs!

I think I have never been so dirty, smelly and cold before. So in all, it was a day to remember in the mud and snow. There was by now almost enough snow on the hill opposite to go skiing!

55

Skip the mystery dog

ANNA WAS A SLIM, MIDDLE-AGED, weathered woman with short grey hair who lived by herself. She had a dog named Skip. I had expressed my concern for her that she lived on her own in a cottage on a piece of land in the bush.

"I don't live alone," she told me passionately. "I come home to my darling Skip every day."

That was so true. A dog can be the most wonderful loyal companion that loves you no matter what.

Skip came from the pound and was supposed to be a neutered male. He was a little brown dog resembling a Chihuahua crossed with some sort of terrier.

The little dog had a temper to match. Once when we had dinner at a friend's place, Skip and Anna were invited as well. Skip was lying under the table guarding Anna's feet while we were eating and chatting away. I happened to move my feet slightly and suddenly Skip took a bite at them.

"Ouch!" I cried. "He bit me!

"I am so sorry for that," Anna said, embarrassed by her companion's bad behaviour. "He's never done that before."

"That's OK," I replied, somewhat annoyed. "I know what some little dogs can be like. He is protecting you."

One day Anna brought Skip into the clinic because he had developed an egg-sized lump between his back legs, and it was getting larger. I had a feel of the softish lump, and it didn't seem to be painful at all. In Australia it is customary to put a tattoo in dogs' and cats' ears when they have been neutered. Strangely enough, Skip didn't have a visible tattoo in his ear. Since he came from the pound we believed he must have been, as it is their policy to desex every animal before passing it on. Maybe the tattoo had faded, or someone had forgotten to put one in.

I had my suspicions, however, that the lump might be a testicle. With the help of my vet nurse, Lyn, I managed to give Skip the intravenous injection in the foreleg that is used to put dogs under for surgery. I had already pre-medicated him with a sedative given under the skin to make him a bit calmer and easier to handle. We still had to put a muzzle on him so we didn't get bitten. When Skip became unconscious, I inserted the plastic tube into his windpipe with the help of Lyn holding his jaws fully open. This would deliver the anaesthetic gas to keep him under for the whole procedure. We put Skip on his back and tied his legs to the table to expose his groin.

When Lyn had clipped and scrubbed the skin clean over the lump ready for surgery, I put a sterile drape with a square hole over the surgical area and carefully incised the skin over the lump. And sure enough, the telltale looks of a typical dog testicle appeared. It was a huge testicle, much bigger than would normally belong to such a tiny dog. It must have slowly grown over the years and become too heavy to stay hidden in the abdomen of the dog any longer. There is always a worry that a retained testicle could become cancerous and the cancer spread in the dog's body. It had to come out at all costs.

After I removed the testicle Anna wanted to keep it in alcohol to show around to her mates. It was a great joke that Skip had had a hidden testicle all these years that had eventually popped out and grown to be so large! It was more of a labrador-sized testicle, not one for a tiny terrier!

✷✷✷

Time went on, and Skip was still fine. Then three years later, out of the blue, I got a call from Anna again.

"You wouldn't believe it," she said. "Skip has had another lump appear in the same place as the previous one! Can I bring him in?"

"I would be very interested to see what is going on this time," I said. I *had* to find out what was happening to Skip. What could this second lump be? A cancer or what?

Anna came in with Skip the next day and I had a good look at the irritable little dog again. I had a good feel of the lump between his legs.

"This lump feels the same as the first one," I explained. "The same softish consistency but a bit smaller. I reckon it is another testicle!"

"This explains why he hasn't got a tattoo in his ear," I continued. "When he arrived at the pound, they naturally thought that he had been neutered somewhere but never got a tattoo for some reason. Skip is a very rare dog indeed!"

I went on to explain to Anna that Skip was a bilateral cryptorchid, which means he had two non-descended testicles that eventually showed up one by one! This is the first and only case I have ever seen like this one. As Skip was getting quite old and decrepit we didn't bother removing the second testicle. I had to put him to sleep a few months later because his ever-worsening arthritis was crippling him.

56

Lucky the water buffalo

BECAUSE I DIDN'T HAVE A shop front, working from home, I had to put ads in the local weekly paper as well as in the phone book. I lived on a five-acre property fifteen kilometres south of Hobart and had built a small clinic there. I made a magnetic veterinary sign that stuck to my car with my mobile number. I also taped up home-printed signs on windows in shopping centres. One of these signs were spotted by what became a long, interesting client relationship and my first and only experience with water buffaloes.

It was close to Christmas, which in these parts is summertime, and nice and not too cold. We had a bit of twilight, since Tasmania is a fair way south. In the middle of cooking dinner (as usual!) my mobile went off.

"Is that the vet?" somebody asked.

"Yes, speaking," I replied curiously. I wondered what this

was all about this time of night. It is usually an emergency.

"I have a water buffalo cow with a calf stuck. It is well and truly jammed, we've tried to pull on it to no avail. Are you able to come out?" the man on the other end asked.

"Has she had calves before?" I asked.

"No, this is the first one."

I had seen many cattle with calving problems but never a buffalo! I had no idea what a buffalo would be like. Why would anyone keep buffaloes in Tasmania? As far as I was concerned, they belonged in the tropics. I had butterflies in my stomach as usual when I was faced with a new challenge. This could be very interesting.

"I will be out ASAP." There went my dinner. I just had to go hungry again.

It was getting dark (as usual!) when I drove the long drive south. I was thinking about this new type of animal and how I would deal with it. Could I treat it as if it was a "normal" cow? There was no time to find out.

Ted's place was a hilly green property nestled in Tasmania's south. The rainfall was quite high normally, and this year had seen a lot, so everything was green. The fencing around the paddocks was substantial, with very high two-metre wire netting. I found out later that Ted also had deer, so he needed the high fences.

The buffalo that needed attention was in some yards further along. To get there we had to carry my heavy equipment that I thought I needed (but it is never enough and several more trips trudging through mud and large heavy gates back to the car were inevitable). Ted opened at least two huge gates in the deep mud, which I remember still today as being a rather arduous task. The ground was really badly mashed up by heavy buffalo hooves all along the way. This was rubber boot country! (Trying to keep my boots from getting sucked off and stumbling on my face is another story!)

It was close to being dark and I could just make out the huge curved-back horns of a black buffalo in a muddy yard. It was a daunting animal indeed but also beautiful.

"Are they quiet to handle?" I asked Ted with trepidation.

"They're not too bad if you don't stir them up," Ted replied. "Most of them are OK."

My gawd! I was excited and scared at the same time! I had never seen such a beast close up like this before. The rear of the buffalo cow had two little feet sticking out. She had a sad look in her eyes, but she also looked a bit wary of me. She held her head stretched out with the wet black nose up, like all buffaloes do.

"The calf may still be alive with a bit of luck, if you only noted a problem this morning," I said. "Can you put her in the crush please so I can have a feel?"

To get the cow into a narrow head bail with those huge wide horns was tricky! They seem to know that their horns are going to get in the way, so they twist their head sideways to fit through. Once the head was through, Ted had to quickly pull the lever to close the sidebars on the bail or she would rush through. She was trapped.

I entered the crush from behind in the heavy mud and had a feel of the pieces sticking out of her behind. I could not detect any foul smell of a dead calf. There was hope the calf was still alive.

"There is no hope of getting this calf out the natural way,"

I stated. "The passage is far too tight. It will have to be a caesarean."

I had no idea how to do a caesarean on a buffalo. I had to extrapolate from a normal cow and hope for the best.

The cattle dose of anaesthetic in the tail vein worked beautifully. After a few minutes the mum-to-be sat down on her chest as I had hoped.

Now came the fun of trying to get needles into that thick hide. A buffalo hide is much thicker than that of a "normal" cow. The needles kept on bending as I placed the local anaesthetic along the left flank where I was about to cut her open. I had to use several needles since they all got blunted and bent.

How these large animals, be they cattle of buffaloes, can survive such big operations in an open paddock or dirty yard is nothing short of amazing. All I can do is shave the hair and scrub the skin with soap and antiseptic. All we have available is buckets of hopefully warmish water. Sometimes the animal is far away in a paddock and already down so it can't be moved anywhere. Water has to be transported in the back of cars in those situations. I have to scrub my hands and arms in the bucket as well as scrubbing the patient. It is not exactly the sterile environment we expect in a surgical theatre.

I wondered if my sharp scalpel was going to get through the immensely tough hide. With a lot of persuasion and pushing I managed to cut a long enough opening in the hide of the left flank to fit a calf through. The rest of the surgery was not much different to the cattle I have done in the past. After I felt for the uterus at arm's length deep inside the flank, I sliced a long cut in it with a new, sharp scalpel blade hidden and tied to my cupped hand. I then reached for the slippery calf deep inside the uterus and grabbed hold of a leg. With Ted's help, I finally managed to pull out the baby calf via the tight opening in the mum's flank! What a wonderful feeling! There was a brand new, living little creature on the ground. Welcome to the world, little fella! The calf instinctively shook his wet newborn head. He was perfectly healthy after all that trauma.

I now had to stitch everything back together. Ted's aged father was there to help, so I got him to quickly wash his hands in the tepid water bucket. This was not really good enough, but I was getting tired hours later and any help would do. I managed to pull out the uterus to be stitched up, and I got Ted's father to hold it up for me. This worked well. My back was now aching from stooping over for several hours.

After the buffalo was put back together it was well after midnight. I drove home covered in mud, blood and faeces. This buffalo was a new experience and I felt good about myself to have done what I had done, but I was also exhausted.

Many months later I asked Ted how everything was going. He said the calf and mum were doing well. There had been no infections or problems at all. Animals' immune systems are incredible. Ted said the calf was as tame as could be and had become part of the family. Ted's young children were all riding him around the place. They called him Lucky.

***

I will always remember when I pulled little Lucky out of the hole I cut in his mum's flanks. Many years have passed since then. The children grew up and Lucky got old and is no more.

57

Dogs and delusions

One of my nicest and most longstanding clients was a middle-aged lady who was breeding labrador retrievers. Betty was divorced and had a teenage son living with her who was mentally challenged and had to go to a special protected workplace. Betty was of medium height, a bit overweight and somewhat plain. She had a nervous giggle. She was unemployed or maybe on a pension. Her parents paid her bills for her, and she had a good car that her father gave her.

I used to do home visits to vaccinate her dogs and puppies. Her home was situated on acreage a fair way from my place. The house was in the middle of a barren, unloved-looking plot of land with a few struggling trees on it. The inside of the house was always clean and tidy. The dogs were kept in a large shed at the back except for the occasional dog in a crate in the kitchen that used to bark like mad when I arrived. It was difficult to have a conversation until the dog settled down.

I always insisted on a cup of tea, which Betty usually managed to produce. We chatted like women do about our private lives after I got to know her a bit better. When I asked her if she had any boyfriends on the go, Betty told me that she had a "stalker". I used to take her answer about the stalker as a bit of a joke between us. Little did I know that the stalker was a real and serious thing indeed to Betty.

After a few years I gradually got to know the true Betty. She had now moved to another house in the same suburb. She told me she had to get away from the stalker who had moved in next door. She also told me that the stalker had broken into her house and urinated on the floor. She pointed to a spot in the lounge room. I started to wonder if things weren't right with Betty. Surely it was one of her dogs that had urinated on the carpet!

A year or so later Betty wanted me to come out and vaccinate all her dogs since they had to go to a kennel. Betty explained that she was pregnant and had to go to hospital. I didn't query this information, guessing it was all in her mind. As I happily got on with vaccinating all her dogs, she started telling me that the stalker had broken into her house, drugged her and had sex with her. And now she was pregnant. I went along with her story. Poor Betty was desperately lonely, and her mind made up a reality that she wished to be true.

Months later she invited me to her engagement party, which was later cancelled. I asked her who she was getting engaged to. She was getting engaged to the stalker, she told me with a smile and a giggle. Whatever happened about her wishful pregnancy? I did not ask.

Betty used to show her dogs, and she was infatuated with one of the judges, a much older married man from interstate. I later found out that she had put an advertisement in one of the big newspapers that she and this judge was going to get married! She had the ad displayed on her Facebook page for everyone to see. Apparently all the dog people knew about Betty and what she had done. The poor dog judge must have been very annoyed over the whole thing. There is a form of delusion that lonely people have because they are so much wanting romance in their lives that they make everything up to the extent they believe it is true.

A year or so later Betty had moved again to a third house in the same suburb again. She explained that the stalker kept on moving in next door, so she had to move. I had a male friend who once came along to the next home visit I had to Betty and her dogs. We had a nice time vaccinating some dogs. In the course of the conversation I asked Betty how her mother was. She used to tell me about her mum and that she visited her regularly. Her mum lived in a suburb near me. We later had a walk around Betty's new garden, commenting on how dry it was, then we went home.

The next day I got a phone call from Betty telling me off for asking about her mum. She said if anything happened to her mum she would blame me. I had to go along with it and say that I was Betty's friend and would not harm her mother.

Yet another week later I got another call from Betty. This time it was about the friend I took with me to see Betty. She said that my friend had been stalking her. I explained that my friend was back in Sydney and that he was not a boyfriend of mine but a longstanding friend only. I realised she was jealous. She replied that the stalking man looked very much like my friend.

I haven't heard from Betty for a couple of years now. Just as well, although she always paid her bills. Dealing with mentally unstable people can have its risks and cause problems.

58

A horse jammed under huge logs

Later on in my career, while I had my own small home-based clinic in southern Tasmania, a woman who we will call June was running a so-called rescue farm. A few unemployed people did this, living on donations and government handouts. June mainly had horses, including a few unwanted or broken-down thoroughbreds. I was happily messing about in my large garden one nice sunny afternoon when my mobile phone went off. I wondered what sort of emergency this was going to be, shuddering with the thought of a nasty horse colic or a poor cow with calving problems.

"Is that the vet?" a stressed female voice asked at the other end.

"Speaking," I answered with apprehension. Butterflies were fluttering around in my stomach, having a lovely time.

"Do you do horses?"

"Yes, what can I do for you?" I thought this had to be a colic for sure. The butterflies went wild!

"Two of my horses have got badly trapped under some fallen logs. We managed to get one of them out, but the other is still stuck. Can you come out ASAP?"

I am a horse lover who has had many myself in the past. I had all sorts of pictures in my mind of the poor horse stuck under these logs. I wondered how bad it was and if it had broken legs and so on. Was it in pain? What would a horse be thinking when it is stuck and can't run away from predators? Their natural instinct is to flee from danger. I wondered what I could do if anything? I couldn't move logs. I was picturing myself somehow performing a euthanasia between the logs.

In the past I have had to euthanise horses in all sorts of places, between rails or on steep hillsides because the owner wants to bury the horse there. Often I have had to take the horse to a pre-dug hole so it would fall into the hole. I had to be careful so I didn't go in with it or end up underneath it. I have had horses rear up high in the air and fall over backwards with a thump after I injected the lethal drug. I have had to inject euthanasia solution on a poor horse with relentless colic pain that wanted to push itself frantically onto me. It can be a very dangerous occupation!

And when I tell people to stand out of the way because of the danger, they go on to inform me that they have had this done before and insist on standing in front of their horse.

After making sure I had all the necessary gear I might need, I hopped in my work vehicle and drove down the fifty winding kilometres to June's place. At least it wasn't raining. I tried not to think of the worst.

As I got out of the car, I introduced myself to an untidy woman, dressed in worn-out jeans and an old T-shirt, who came up to me smoking a cigarette. There was a small, curious child close by. The woman thanked me for coming out. She first explained that her beloved animals were rescued from being put down. She told me that kind people were giving her hay for the horses and that the other local vet clinic was really nice and attended to them free of charge. Was this a hint?

A good life on other people's expense I thought. Collect all these unwanted animals around you and get donations to live on. Some "collectors" as I call them, collect old cows, sheep and pigs. On the other side of the coin, we kill them to eat. Often some people keep curiosities, such as sheep born with stunted legs or a cow born with only three legs. Would it not be more humane to kill animals that live a life in pain, given that we kill the healthy ones to eat? Is it not like having people with deformities in a circus to live on their abnormal looks?

June looked to be in her late thirties and had young children running about. Her house was a small weatherboard building. It looked old and dilapidated and had not seen any paint for a long time. She was obviously unemployed. She kept on smoking on a cigarette. *They have money for cigarettes while everybody else pays for her animals*, I thought.

The farm was divided into a couple of grassy paddocks, and there was a stand of old huge poplar trees in a wet gully at the corner of the horses' paddock.

I could make out some enormous logs lying on the ground criss-crossing each other. June and I walked down towards the trees. I saw the head and ears of a brown horse sticking up between several huge logs. The logs must have been 25 metres long. The horse, a thoroughbred gelding, was bright and alert and had a rug on. His hindquarters sat on the wet soft ground. The two stretched-out front legs held up the front end of the horse. He held his head up in a normal position. The horse had made several attempts to get up, but his rear was firmly jammed between two very long poplar logs that ran lengthwise on either side of his body, forming a V at the hindquarters. The gap between the two logs was just too narrow for his broad hindquarters to fit through. How amazing that none of the logs had come down on his withers or even crushed him completely!

There was nothing I could do to help him. June had offered him water between the logs. I was totally at a loss at this horrendous scene. I had never encountered anything like this before. At least the horse seemed calm.

We had to find someone with seriously heavy equipment to try and move the huge logs, which must have weighed several thousand kilograms each. Chain-sawing them off could be tricky; they were very thick and there was a risk that they could roll and crush the animal if parts were sawn off.

All I could do was wait to see if we could get him freed and then see if he was able to get up and walk away. Or the possibility was that he would have to be euthanised if he couldn't or if he was too seriously injured.

Several hours went by. Over time a crowd of people formed willing to help but nobody could really do anything. Finally, they got hold of a man with a tractor with a scoop. He tried to lift one log with the scoop and direct it away from the horse. The huge tractor tyres sank and slipped in the deep wet mud. After many tries from different angles the log finally budged.

The poor horse had been in the same sitting position now for who knows how many hours. He could have been there all night. We went up to his head and tried to encourage him to get up. After so many earlier tries he had almost given up. His legs must have been cramping after sitting in the same position for so long, probably all night and most of the day. Large animals get nerve damage when too much pressure from their bodyweight is exerted on them.

The horse stuck between the heavy logs – amazing that he was not injured!

Yet, after a few minutes and a few tries the brown gelding stood up as if he had never been stuck in the same sitting position for so many hours. He walked away without a limp, without a scratch! It seemed like a miracle. I tried to hide the tears that rolled down my cheeks. The soft, muddy ground that had caused the huge poplars to fall down in the wind in the first place had also saved him. The deep mud helped by padding the bony parts of his legs. I gave the horse a thorough check-over and could not find anything wrong anywhere. I gave him a gentle pat on the neck, whispering to him what a good job he had done staying calm all that time.

Five hours after arriving, I drove home without having had to do anything much more than watch. This was an event I would remember forever. June rang me the next day to say thank you. Needless to say, I never did get paid for my time, but to be part of such an extraordinary event with such a happy ending was worth it anyway.

59

The evil client

You have to deal with all sorts of people when you work with the public. Most are nice, but some are not so nice.

One day I received a call from a female we shall call Jenny. Her dog had a sore paw, she told me. She did not have a car to take the dog to a clinic, so she asked me if I could come to her place instead.

When I arrived after a long drive up a country track, the dog, a hairy, middle-sized crossbred, looked fine. It was wagging its tail and was happy to see the vet. I examined the whole dog from head to tail as usual and found that a toenail on one of the fore paws was broken up near the quick, the area where the nail grows from. This is a common occurrence, and the treatment is to remove as much of the remaining nail as possible, so this is what I successfully managed to do.

I bandaged the foot lightly and gave Jenny some antibiotics to give to the dog over the next five days.

When I handed the bill to Jenny, who was on a pension, she said she only had money to pay for the antibiotics. I advised her she could pay off the remaining account later. I left wondering if I would ever get paid for the home visit.

After a week of not hearing from Jenny, I sent her a reminder for the outstanding account. This is where the story gets a twist.

When Jenny got the reminder account, she phoned me and said that the dog had nearly died from the bandage and that if I ever asked her for the money again, she would contact the Veterinary Board and complain! I told her I was sorry that she perceived there had been a problem.

The next day I got yet another call, this time from a man saying he was the ex-boyfriend of Jenny. He informed me that Jenny was on medication for some mental disorder and apologised for her bad behaviour towards me. He said that *he* would pay the bill. I thanked him for that and hung up. I never heard from him or Jenny again.

Needless to say, I never got paid for this job. It wasn't worth the trouble and stress to have to deal with the Veterinary Board, since they are obliged to deal with every complaint, no matter how silly or minor. Sadly, this was not going to be the last time that I never got paid for work I had done!

60

The wake

THE STRANGEST AND MOST BIZARRE veterinary home visit I ever did was with an elderly dog. I used to attend a local choir once a week. I loved singing. I also got to know people in the area. Peter and Helen were living near me, and I got to know them at the meetings. I mentioned to them that I was a vet. Many months later I had a call from Peter.

"I hate to ask you this," he said with a hesitant voice. "My old dog is no longer mobile, and I am afraid he will have to be put down. He is in a lot of pain, and I can't stand seeing him suffer anymore."

"I am sad to hear that," I replied with concern. "How old is he and what type of dog is he?"

"Cooper is a hound, and he is fifteen," Peter informed me. "He has been struggling around for some time, and he spends most of his life lying down resting."

The wake

I always found it hard to know what to say when a person asked me to put their beloved pet down. "Were you thinking of a home visit or in the clinic?" I asked.

"A home visit please."

"What time and what day were you thinking of?" I enquired tentatively, knowing very well how painful this question would be.

"Can you please come this Saturday at 10 am?" Peter asked hopefully.

"Yes, no problem."

"And can you please be there exactly at ten?" This question perplexed me a bit. I always try to arrive at home visits at the agreed time, but sometimes that can be difficult, especially if I have to travel some distance. Since Peter lived nearby, that shouldn't present a problem.

"I will try and be there exactly at ten," I replied. I was to find out on Saturday why the exact time was so important.

Saturday morning arrived. The usual butterflies started to flutter in my guts. Euthanasias are never much fun. Things can sometimes go wrong. I have had to do them on a dog hiding under a bush. I often had to do them on the floor inside a dark home. Once I couldn't find the vein in the dark, with the stressed owners abusing me and crying wildly. Once I had to inject the dog into the chest when I had tried both leg veins and made them unusable. The worst case ever was in the clinic, with the owner holding the dog. I missed the vein on the foreleg slightly and some of the lethal solution went outside the vein under the skin. This can be disastrous, causing excitement instead of unconsciousness. The dog started howling loudly with the owner crying and shouting at me *do something, do something!* It was the most horrible instant of my veterinary career! But that is another story – back to Peter and his dog Cooper.

I was met at the door by Peter when I arrived at a quarter to ten. I already felt pretty bad as it was. I was to feel even worse when Peter told me what was really going on! He told me that his wife Helen had died of cancer recently. He had decided to hold a wake with family and friends at the same time Cooper was being put down!

As I entered the lounge room, there were about twenty-five people sitting around it, as if in an amphitheatre. I felt their piercing stares. I didn't know where to look. I was waiting for the lions and the battle to begin!

In the centre of the room Cooper was lying down quietly, with his head resting on the floor. My mouth was getting drier. I felt as if I was choking! What if something went wrong with all these spectators watching and judging every move I made as well?

Cooper was a nice dog, and he didn't even lift his head when I carefully crouched down beside him. I collected myself for the very emotional task ahead. There was a power point nearby so I could plug in the electric clippers. The old dog didn't react at all as I clipped the short hairs on the foreleg. *So far so good,* I thought. *If he didn't mind the clippers, maybe he won't mind the needle.*

Thankfully everything went as planned, and Cooper went to sleep without any unexpected complications. I gently stroked his head to comfort him, and to ask his forgiveness for putting him to sleep forever. Finally I stood up to leave, gave Peter a hug and said goodbye.

When I got back home, I eventually settled down for the rest of the day. I hoped this would be the last time for this sort of stressful home euthanasia.

61

Dandy

Some of the things I experienced as a veterinarian will stay in my mind forever. This day was going to be one of those instances. When you work for yourself you should really be glad when you get work, but I was sipping on a cup of tea when my mobile phone went off with its irritating noise that annoys us so often these days. It was early afternoon.

"Margareta speaking," I answered, trying to hide my annoyance over being interrupted with my cup of tea. It was Irene, one of my trusted long-term customers.

"Dandy is not herself, doc. She's standing in one spot and has been constantly pawing at the ground for over an hour. Then she lies down for long periods as well." Dandy was her beloved ten-year-old chestnut mare. She was very quiet and lovely to look at and handle.

"Have you just fed her hay by any chance?" I asked.

Sometimes after eating a bit of hay some horses will show signs of a mild choke and be uncomfortable for a while after.

"She hasn't had any hay since this morning," Irene replied. She sounded really distressed. It was now 2 pm.

"What you are describing is colic or belly ache really," I said as carefully as I could as not to upset Irene. "The cause of colic symptoms are many and varied."

I didn't want to worry Irene unnecessarily by elaborating on the subject and going into the more serious possibilities.

"I'll be over straight away" I said hastily. As I was driving, I went over in my mind the different scenarios for colic and what I would do. I had attended many colics before and while colic can be mild indigestion that can resolve itself, most of the cases I had attended had sadly been severe and ended in me putting the horse down. Was this going to be one of those? I shuddered at the thought.

Luckily the travel distance was not far, so I arrived in fifteen minutes. Irene met me at the gate; she was close to hysterical with worry and her face looked drawn.

"I've had this mare since a foal and love her dearly," she said with tears rolling down her face. "I can't stand the thought of losing her."

I tried to calm her down and also to hide the butterflies I had in my own stomach. I hated the thought of maybe having to tell her that the horse had to be put down, relaying back to my previous cases.

At a distance I spotted the chestnut mare lying down, apparently peacefully, in her paddock. Horses rarely lie down to rest in the afternoon. She was a well-fed, healthy-looking mare and was very quiet, allowing me to examine her without any trouble while lying down. I could listen to her heart with my stethoscope on her chest and took note that it was of a normal rate and rhythm, around forty *lub-dub* beats per minute. I lifted her soft, velvety lips up slightly to examine her mucous membranes; they were pink and moist, and that is always a good sign.

"I am going to give Dandy a potent painkiller into her jugular vein to start with," I told Irene. "This helps to assess the severity of her pain." (If the painkiller does not help, it is likely the horse needs surgery for a twisted gut – which is rarely done anyway; it's usually a case for euthanasia.)

"We have to get her up off the ground first so I can listen to her belly." I grabbed the halter and pulled on the mare's head. We used our feet to push on her rear end as well. She stood up after a few tries.

I put my stethoscope against her smooth, rounded belly on different areas and listened intensely. I could not hear any gurgling sounds at all on any part of her abdomen. Normally I could hear a swooshing sound as liquids were mixing inside the intestines. No sounds meant no good. This could mean that the digestive tract was not working as it should. Indeed, it was not working at all.

All this put together pointed me to a simple bowel impaction, but sometimes more serious events can start off looking like that. I now gave the mare an intravenous painkiller in the jugular vein as planned. The mare cooperated nicely this time.

"We just have to wait a few minutes to see the response. If the colic is mild Dandy should be looking as if normal again and start picking at the grass," I said, hoping for the best.

Unfortunately, this did not happen. Dandy continued to

paw desperately at the ground. The painkiller did not work. The pain was too great.

"I need you to get two buckets of warm water," I told Irene. "I have to tube her and give warm water directly into her stomach. This may help shift the blockage." To do this I usually have to put a nose twitch on the top lip, which is a very mobile and easily accessible body part of a horse. It seems made for this purpose. I then feed the tube into the left nostril towards the neck. The horse has to swallow it so it doesn't go down the windpipe. This can be a fairly simple procedure, or it can be a nightmarish one. This time it was going to be the nightmarish one.

Dandy had been wormed a few times in the past via mouth and did not like being touched at all around her lips. It proved impossible to get a twitch on her top lip. She was throwing her head in all directions and came close to rearing up to avoid being touched around her mouth. Horses are dangerous animals and can easily knock you out with their head or worse, strike you with a front foot with lightning speed. I met a horse woman a long time ago with a stitched-up lip that had been split by a hoof. I nearly got hit once myself when vaccinating my own yearling!

"I will have to sedate her via the jugular vein again so we can get the twitch on her," I informed Irene, who had settled down a bit now. After the sedative started to work and Dandy's head started to drop down, I could put the twitch on her lip without any trouble. It consisted of a loop of cord at the end of a polypipe, placed over the top lip and twisted tight. This made the horse concentrate on the nose instead of anything else that was happening.

I placed the plastic stomach tube in the warm water to make it more pliable, since it happened to be a freezing cold day. After gently inserting it into the left nostril and sliding it up Dandy's nose I felt the junction where the windpipe and the oesophagus (food pipe) cross over. She luckily swallowed instantly, and I could push the tube down all the way to her stomach. I could see the tube on the neck through the skin as I slid it down. If it was in the windpipe it would not be visible like that.

Dandy stood there with the long tube all the way into her stomach and the other end hanging out of her nostril as if mesmerised. Now all we had to do was to pour down the warm water via a funnel!

"I will put some liquid paraffin oil down the tube after the water as a marker to see if anything comes through her intestines later," I informed Irene. "You can have a look later tonight if you can see oil on her backside."

Now it was up to the mare to sort herself out, with the water helping to push the impacted ingesta along.

The mare was still uncomfortable. I told Irene this was normal and that it took several hours for the treatment to work and to be patient. So I went home, hoping this would fix the problem so I could hop in the hot bath and put my feet up for the day and start cooking dinner.

At 8 pm the phone rang. I was in the middle of serving myself a hot meal. I wondered what would ensue next. I bet myself it would be Irene.

That would be my luck. Irene sounded more than a bit tiddly and sentimental from alcohol.

"She's no better," she sobbed. "She's still pawing the ground like mad and has dug a hole in her stable shed. She has to be put down."

I explained to Irene over and over that the treatment takes all night to work and to be patient.

"She is no better. She is in a lot of pain. She has to be put down," she whined. Irene repeated herself over and over. The alcohol was doing the talking.

I have had to deal with inebriated customers before. You can't get through to them and I hate it with a vengeance. They can't think rationally. Their judgement is blurred by the alcohol. So what could I do now?

Irene insisted with a slurred voice that I come over and euthanise the mare. I did not know what was the right thing to do in this case, should I refuse or what? What would other vets do? I was in two minds as what to do but decided I had better go and see what was going on with the mare.

I drove back in the cold dark night. Irene met me at the gate to the mare's paddock. She was unstable on her feet as she opened the gate to let me in. Her slurred speech made me more and more annoyed. I hate alcohol and what it does to people. Emotions take over and common sense goes out the window. Irene kept on repeating that the mare had not improved at all and was in a lot of pain.

Dandy was lying down when we approached her in the dark. There was a big hole in the ground where she had been standing. After I checked her over again, she got up by herself. Irene was still adamant that I should put her down. I wondered if she would regret it in the morning when she was sober.

I decided to give Dandy a sedative first, since we were on a muddy hillside in the dark with only a torch and an inebriated owner to hold the lead rope. *Maybe Irene should have a sedative instead,* I thought.

As I was trying to insert the small needle into Dandy's jugular, the mare went wild all of a sudden and started running around in circles at the end of the lead rope, knocking Irene over onto the ground. I could not go near the mare; she had become very needle-shy at this stage. I had difficulty seeing anything, being blinded by the torchlight. I decided that it was too dangerous to do anything more this dark night. I could not risk anyone getting hurt. Maybe this was for the best anyway. The mare would just have to suffer until the morning.

I went back home and had difficulty sleeping after all the excitement. I was relieved that Irene hadn't got seriously hurt. I actually felt pleased that we had to abandon the whole thing.

In the morning at first daylight Irene rang me and said, with some shame in her voice, that the mare appeared normal and was eating her hay as usual. Dandy never did look back after that. This was many years ago. Maybe the universe intervened to save the beautiful chestnut mare. Dandy was not ready to go yet. I sometimes wonder.

THE END

www.ingramcontent.com/pod-product-compliance
Lightning Source LLC
Chambersburg PA
CBHW030547080526
44585CB00012B/293